Praise for
I WAS CARLOS CAST

"In the beginning, I thought this was a book of metafiction or magical realism. It is something else entirely: a discussion between new friends, a dreamy travelogue, a teaching. It is a magical mystery tour in humility, truth, death, betrayal, forgiveness, the envelopment of nature, written as clearly and powerfully as a French Pyrenees river where Goodman and Castaneda stop to swim and talk." — **Karla Kuban**, author of *Marchlands*

"From the Pyrenees to the Amazon rain forest, Martin Goodman vividly describes Castaneda's most powerful and important teachings—the nature of the journey beyond death." — **Alberto Villoldo, Ph.D.**, author of *Shaman, Healer, Sage* and *Dance of the Four Winds*

"A marvelous book with rich teachings that particularly touch the heart of death—and, thus, life itself." — **Thom Hartmann**, author of *The Last Hours of Ancient Sunlight*

"The Old Trickster has done it again! Having stirred up a storm of controversy and speculation in his lifetime with his astonishing tales of sorcerers and shamans, Castaneda now makes a posthumous appearance in Martin Goodman's story. But now Goodman plays the role of bewildered student, to Carlos's amused and provocative pronouncements." — **Ralph Metzner, Ph.D.**, author of *The Unfolding Self*

"To invite someone like Carlos Castaneda into one's life, especially when he's dead, is asking for it. Martin Goodman, who barely escaped death in Amazonas, gets the full treatment from the old master and learns a thing or two to his own and the reader's advantage. To Castaneda's, too: I reckon he's in better form than ever before." — **Francis Huxley**, author of *The Way of the Sacred*

"This is an absorbing tale, which succeeds at entertaining while it informs. Goodman, writing with warmth and humor, has woven a story of a modern day shaman's apprentice, cast adrift amid the turbulent outer zones of consensus reality before returning once again to solid ground. It is a delightful read, and I recommend it highly." — **Charles S. Grob, M.D.**, professor of psychiatry at the UCLA School of Medicine

THREE RIVERS PRESS • NEW YORK

I WAS CARLOS CASTANEDA

THE AFTERLIFE DIALOGUES

MARTIN GOODMAN

FOR JAMES

Published by Three Rivers Press, New York, New York. Member of
the Crown Publishing Group.

Random House, Inc. New York, Toronto, London, Sydney, Auckland
www.randomhouse.com

THREE RIVERS PRESS is a registered trademark and the
Three Rivers Press colophon is a trademark of Random House, Inc.

Printed in the United States of America

Design by Deborah Kerner

Library of Congress Cataloging-in-Publication Data
Goodman, Martin.
    I was Carlos Castaneda : the afterlife dialogues / Martin
Goodman—1st ed.
        p. cm.
    1. Castaneda, Carlos, 1931– 2. Castaneda, Carlos, 1931–
(Spirit) I. Castaneda, Carlos, 1931– (Spirit) II. Title.
BF1311.C37 G66 2001
133.9'3—dc21   00-027684

ISBN 0-609-80763-3

10 9 8 7 6 5 4 3 2 1

First Edition

CONTENTS

ACKNOWLEDGMENTS

At the close of a ceremony sometime after the events described in this book, the participants held a thanksgiving. Thanks were given to friends, and also to those who had made lives hell for a while. They were all part of the history that had brought us to the present moment, and that moment was absolutely fine. Worth all the thanks we could ever give.

So the distinction between friends and enemies was dropped, and everybody was thanked by name. When we ran out of names we moved on to species, so even mosquitoes and malarial parasites got a mention.

Many people are part of the fabric of this book in some way. They have my thanks, even though they are not necessarily named here. Names are withheld to honor their privacy most of all. For the same reason, I have disguised, renamed, omitted, and merged characters in the narrative. People are free to declare their own interests and involvement in the story told here. I intend that they also be free to keep their anonymity.

This book could not have happened without my earlier practice in breaking bounds. My years in Scotland introduced me to an alternative and vigorous take on culture, and I thank the Scottish Arts Council for their generous funding for my writing career.

In teaching terms, my weekly tutorials with Professor Peter Geach engaged me with a master of Socratic dialogue.

Professor Geoffrey Hill brazenly confounded lecture halls filled with students who wanted their literature simplified or explained in psychological terms, and showed the way to wonder. I appreciated this renowned poet's advice that my own writing must first be grounded in the study of those who have gone before me. It's hard to break the bounds without recognizing them.

James Broughton's first gift to me was a copy of his *Androgyne Journal*, a manual for transcending all known categories of wonder. He led life on his own terms, and those terms were dictated by love. Even in illness his encouragement for my writing was constant, and I have enjoyed trying to implement some of the lessons he gave. He now blesses heaven as well as Earth.

Jeanette Watson gave inspirational and truly generous support at a crisis point in my career, an act that helped make this book possible.

My thanks to Christobel Haward, whose readiness to gift her little house in the French Pyrenees ultimately saw me in place for the events in this book. My thanks to Pam Clark and Mel Clark, and Madame Rosa Capela, for their care for me and my home in the village. It is a magical land.

As is my home in mountains near Santa Fe, New Mexico, where I am writing now. The land here has nurtured this book.

On the morning I was to begin writing, a coyote stepped out of the surrounding woodland and paced around the yard. I have glimpsed coyotes' bodies gliding between the trees, and I wake regularly to the primeval chorus of their celebration howls as they gather in the night outside our house, but this is the only such daytime sighting in my years here. I took the appearance as a special blessing on the nature of this book, and so I thank the coyote.

When I walked from the house to begin that day's writing, I came up to the "bothy." This is a sublime and beautiful writing studio gifted to the land by Emma Thompson and designed by Greg Wise—the architectural work itself an astonishing gift. Greg speaks of the design as a "fallen tepee," for the structure is angled for its roof to rest on a lattice of massive and graceful hand-hewn beams as it shoots high to embrace the view of mountains. The building redefines Santa Fe style in a most appropriate way, for it embodies the union of sky and Earth that is so strong a feature of the high-altitude life here. It is a blessing to have worked here.

My thanks to Lynette Herring, Dr. Romig, and the staff of St. Vincent's Hospital here in Santa Fe. Without their urgent care and expertise I would not have lived to finish this tale.

Not all stories are meant to be told. After writing the first episodes, I set this book aside. It seemed enough to have survived the personal experience, and there was still a lot to learn from the lessons I had received. I doubted my strength to bring this particular book into being and thus engage with the energy of the world. So I thank my mother, Kay O'Neill, for reading that early portion and urging me to continue. You might notice from the nature of this book what an unusual mother I have. She was my first lesson in breaking bounds.

Toinette Lippe recognized the merit in that early portion, and worked selflessly and resourcefully with my agent Lorraine Kisly to bring it to its publishing home. My editor Patricia Gift moved swiftly to create that publishing home at Three Rivers Press. They are my blithe spirits. I couldn't have written this book without their encouragement and support, so I thank them very much.

My thanks to Ralph Metzner and Dr. Charles Grob, who gave early and expert help in putting my experiences of ayahuasca into perspective. Also to Colleen Kelly, Robert Ott, George Greer, and Requa Tolbert for their inspired listening and pleasing counsel, and Mac Hawley for his reminiscences of Castaneda that should have prepared me better for my meeting.

My partner James Thornton has led me to break more bounds than I knew existed. He encouraged me on the bold early steps of this journey, accompanied me, protected me, and nursed me. Over our shared daily ritual of pots of tea he brought his intellectual brilliance, his mystical experience, his keen intuition and infinite love and care to many conversations. Sharing life with him, it isn't possible to remain in the miasma of unresolved conflicts. For me, he is the reason that a phoenix can rise from the ashes.

My thanks and respect to Carlos Castaneda. When it comes to breaking bounds, he leads the field. I appreciate the techniques and truths about writing and life he has shown me.

The most a book can wish for is to keep the reader reading, and to be wrapped in that person's life with the breath of the closing sentence. For the power of reading as an alchemical act I thank you the reader.

Life Before Death—A Brief Introduction
to Carlos Castaneda

In February 1998 I received a curious and completely unexpected invitation—would I like to interview Carlos Castaneda? To the uninitiated, the invitation will mean nothing. But those who came of age in the Sixties counterculture will recognize that it was like being invited to peruse the Cretan Minotaur.

Carlos Castaneda stands alongside Timothy Leary as one of the great avatars—and one of the great enigmas—of the psychedelic age. In 1968 Castaneda published *The Teachings of Don Juan*, describing his apprenticeship in the deserts of Mexico to an Indian shaman, and his induction through mind-altering substances into "the Yaqui way of knowledge."

Like Herman Hesse's *Steppenwolf* and Aldous Huxley's *The Doors of Perception*, *The Teachings of Don Juan* and its sequels became essential reading for a legion of seekers after truth—guidebooks into a fantastic and exotic world beyond the dull grind of materialism. And long after the first generation of fans had moved on to more pragmatic concerns—mortgages, families, tax returns—the books continued to sell. Since 1968, the works of Carlos Castaneda have sold more than eight million copies in seventeen different languages, totally unhindered by the fierce debate about whether Don Juan really existed or was simply a figure of Castaneda's imagination. No less a mystery was Castaneda himself. "The art of the hunter," Don Juan had taught, "is to become inaccessible," and it was a maxim that Castaneda had observed with an almost religious dedication for thirty years, forsaking public appearances, refusing almost all interviews, leading the life of a recluse.

But now, I was told, there had been a mysterious and dramatic change of heart. After years of inaccessibility, Castaneda had emerged into the public eye, bringing with him for the first time what he claimed was the most important facet of Don Juan's teachings—a system of physical movements known as "magical passes." He was prepared to lift the shroud of secrecy and talk to the world.

A date was provisionally set for me to meet him in Los Angeles. I was told that he would countenance no photographs, no tape-recording equipment. I would be allowed only to take notes, as he had taken notes during his years of tutelage at the feet of Don Juan. "A recording," Castaneda had told the *Los Angeles Times* in 1995 in a rare conversation, "is a way of fixing you in time. The only thing a sorcerer will not do is be stagnant. The stagnant world, the stagnant picture, those are the antitheses of the sorcerer."

Then the date was changed. And changed again. Castaneda, I was told, was "on retreat" in the Mexican desert. When—if—he returned, I would be notified. In late March, I left for California on other business. But the call never came. There was a simple reason. At the time that I was sitting in a hotel room in Los Angeles, Castaneda was not in Mexico at all. He was three miles away from me in his Westwood home, dying of liver cancer.

Carlos Castaneda died, at the age of seventy-two, on April 27. But, peculiarly, it was to be another two months before the news of his death became public.

There was no announcement, no press report, no funeral or service of any kind. According to the Culver City mortuary that handled his remains, his body was cremated at once, his ashes spirited away to the Mexican desert.

In death, as in life, Castaneda remained inscrutable. When, eventually, the news of his death leaked out to the press, two British newspapers ran obituaries, alongside photographs of a man who was not Carlos Castaneda. His friends drew a veil of silence over the death, refusing to comment. In a statement to the press, his agents, Toltec Artists, would say only that "In the tradition of the shamans of his lineage, Carlos Castaneda left this world in full awareness."

A key aspect of the teachings of Don Juan, as recounted by Carlos Castaneda, was the necessity of the "self" to die. "It is imperative to leave aside what [Don Juan] called 'personal history,'" Castaneda told the Chilean magazine *Uno Mismo* in 1997. "To get away from 'me' is something extremely annoying and difficult. What the shamans like Don Juan seek is a state of fluidity where the personal 'me' does not count." For Castaneda, "the personal me" was a subject of constant fluctuation and revision.

By his own account, Castaneda was born on December 25, 1935, in São Paulo, Brazil. His mother died when he was seven and he was raised by his father, a professor of literature whom Castaneda supposedly regarded with a mixture of fondness and contempt— a shadow of the man he would subsequently meet in Don Juan. "I am my father," Castaneda told *Time* magazine in his first—and last—major interview in 1973. "Before I met Don Juan, I would spend years sharpening my pencils and then getting a headache every time I sat down to write. Don Juan taught me that's stupid. If you want to do something, do it impeccably, and that's all that matters." He claimed to have been educated in Buenos Aires and sent to America in 1951. He traveled to Milan, where he studied sculpture, before returning to America and enrolling at UCLA to study anthropology.

In fact, American immigration records indicate that Castaneda was born not in 1935, but in 1925—not in Brazil, but in Cajamarca, Peru. His father was not a university professor, but a goldsmith. His mother died when he was twenty-four. And while it was true that he had studied painting and sculpture, this was not in Milan, but at the National Fine Art School in Peru. Arriving in America in 1951, he studied creative writing at Los Angeles City College before enrolling in an anthropology course at UCLA in 1959.

The following year, he traveled to the Mexico-Arizona desert, intending to study the medicinal use of certain plants among local Indians. At a bus station in the town of Nogales in Arizona, he would later write, he met the man he called Don Juan. For the psychedelic generation, it was the equivalent of Stanley stumbling into a jungle clearing and discovering Livingstone, the young John Lennon bumping into Paul McCartney at a church fete in Woolton.

According to Castaneda, Don Juan Matus was a Yaqui Indian nagual, or leader of a party of sorcerers—the last in a line stretching back to the time of the Toltecs, the pre-Hispanic Indians who inhabited the central and northern regions of Mexico a thousand years ago. Under the guidance of the Yaqui sage, Castaneda was introduced to the psychotropic substances of peyote, jimsonweed, and "the little smoke," a preparation made from Psilocybe mushrooms that had been dried and aged for a year. Under the influence of these drugs, the bemused anthropologist underwent a series of bizarre encounters, with columns of singing light, a bilingual coyote, and a 100-foot-tall gnat—"the guardian of the other world"—manifestations of the "powers," or impersonal forces, that a man of knowledge must learn to use.

The Teachings of Don Juan: A Yaqui Way of Knowledge was first published in 1968 as an anthropological thesis by the University of California Press. A year later—repackaged in a psychedelic dust jacket—it was published by a mainstream company. It became an immediate counterculture hit, prompting an exodus of would-be apprentice sorcerers to the deserts of Mexico in search of Don Juan—or at least good drugs.

A Separate Reality, published in 1971, was more of the same—a giant gnat circles around Castaneda, and he sees Don Juan's face transformed into a ball of glowing light—as the old Indian inducted Castaneda into the so-called second cycle of apprenticeship. These experiences were not just psychedelic, magical mystery tours. The use of drugs, Castaneda explained, was Don Juan's way of leading his pupil to "see" the world outside the cultural and linguistic constraints of Western rationalism, unencumbered by conditioned preconceptions or the taint of personal history.

Drugs were not in themselves the destination, he explained in *Journey to Ixtlan,* which was published in 1973; they were merely one route to the destination, to be discarded once this fundamental shift in perception had been achieved. *Journey to Ixtlan* won Castaneda his Ph.D. from UCLA. It also made him a millionaire.

By now, doubts about the authenticity of Castaneda's accounts had begun to multiply. It was one thing for him to refuse to divulge the identity and whereabouts of the Yaqui sage (Don Juan, he always made clear, was a pseudonym that he used to protect his teacher's privacy), but quite another for him to refuse to let his field notes be examined by other anthropologists. But whatever the doubts about the book's provenance, even the most skeptical critics agreed that they were powerful parables about the search for personal enlightenment, "remarkable works of art," as the author Joyce Carol Oates described them.

Shortly before Castaneda's death, his agent delivered to his publisher the manuscript of his last book, *The Active Side of Infinity*. Read in the light of his death, the book has a distinctly valedictory air. Reappraising his encounters with Don Juan, Castaneda reiterates that "the total goal" of shamanic knowledge is preparation for facing the "definitive journey— the journey that every human being has to take at the end of his life" to the region that shamans called "the active side of infinity."

And, then, the journey back to life again?

Soon after Castaneda's death was announced, the Internet was buzzing with accounts from people whom he had supposedly visited in their dreams. Now, Martin Goodman brings us the resurrected Castaneda. Having reconstituted his body in the mountains, Castaneda steps down from the heights of the French Pyrenees. He has issues of his past life to resolve, while evoking powers of sorcery and storytelling to alert Goodman to the magical art of living. The Castaneda of these "Afterlife Dialogues," fresh with lessons and perspectives from his passage beyond death, conjures leaps of credibility reminiscent of one of the most persistent characters of twentieth-century literature . . . the Don Juan of Castaneda's own books.

With Castaneda assuming the role of Don Juan, Goodman is left in the young Castaneda's highly polished shoes.

Publication of this book leaves him open to praise, to thanks, and to criticism. He might find guidance in Castaneda's response to his critics.

That response was always the same. Castaneda was writing about states of mind and perception outside the normal conventions of academia, so the normal terms of reference did not apply. Sorcerers, he said, have only one point of reference: "infinity."

He would continue repeating the same mantra to the very end.

"I invented nothing."

—MICK BROWN

Crazy old men are essential to society.

Otherwise young men have no suitable models.

—JAMES BROUGHTON

I WAS
CARLOS
CASTANEDA

1

THE MEETING

Lightning jags above the Pyrenean mountains, thunder roars, and death takes on new meaning. It is appropriate that the first time I see the man he stands at the foot of the full-size crucifix that borders the road just outside the village. But then everything he does is appropriate.

Do I recognize him, this man who fought shy of cameras all his life? Of course not. His book jackets carry no image of him. I found his first book so disturbing I never read another. Millions bought his every book, but not me.

Then he died. On April 27, 1998. It was some two months before the death was reported, and about two months after then that we meet.

August 21, to be precise.

I'm jumping ahead of myself, but then I'm excited. It's not that he came back from the dead. That's wild enough, but he'll explain it. It's that he chose to come back to me.

The first drops of rain fall. They bounce off his head, and give an extra sheen to the silver hair with its curls drawn back across his scalp. I stop on my walk—not because he looks at me, because he doesn't. He has never seen me before, yet he yells my name out loud against the thunderclaps as he looks up at the naked body of the crucified Christ.

"Martin!"

It's a cry for help. I do nothing but remain where I am as the rain falls.

"Come here and look at this!"

I step up to his side, and we both raise our heads toward the face of Jesus.

"Tell me what's wrong about this, and what's right."

"Is this a riddle?" I ask.

"The only riddle is why I am asking you, and not telling you."

"It's wrong that Jesus was killed?" I suggest.

"You have a simple mind. Maybe that's a virtue in you. Can you absorb all that I am going to tell you? We'll see. First I will tell you what is wrong about this statue. It is pathetic that this crucifix is here. People paid good money to have this piece of wood carved, painted, and erected. What purpose does it serve? Every time they come and go along this road, they are faced with death. Christ is not about dying. He is about eternal life. Not death, but resurrection. If people want a symbol by the side of the road, then let them build an empty tomb. At least such a structure could shelter passersby from the rain. Come on, Martin. We will go to your home and get dry."

He shakes his head to sling water from his hair into my face, then starts off down the road into the village. I am impressed by his language. His voice is gentle, with a slight trace of an accent to give it distinction; I presume the accent comes from nearby Spain, and the flow of his words is beau-

tiful. There is no pause, but softness of delivery gives polish
to every word. His skin is tanned in depth, it has the color
and texture of a local's, but his whole air of being is cos-
mopolitan.

"How do you know my name?"

"Is that what is important? How somebody knows your
name? I use your name because I am talking to you. It is
important that you listen to what I have to say rather than
waste time wondering why I say it. We are speaking of
Christ. There is time to consider you later. You now know
what is bad about hanging this dead body beside the road for
all to see. This morbid fascination with death kills the spirit.
But tell me, what is good about it?"

"The craftsmanship?"

"Nonsense. You go past this statue on your walk every
day. Do you ever stop and stare at it as I was doing?"

"Sometimes. Not for so long."

"That's fine, as it happens. There is not so much to see.
I am a sculptor myself, trained in Italy, so you can take my
word for the quality of the piece. But you can never know
this much for yourself, not about sculpture or anything, any
work of man or nature, unless you spend time staring into it.
Tune yourself to where you're looking, Martin. Open wide
and see if there is a message for you there. If there is, you will
know it from your eyes. They will vibrate. You will take in the
energy of its creator. If you stare at a tree or a flower, you take
in the energy of the universe. Stare at a statue, and you take
in the energy of the sculptor. The devotion in that sculptor
was slight. There is little that is universal there. But there
was some care as he formed this image of the male human
body. The male nude. You can see he ran his hands over
the wooden skin. What value there is in this sculpture is in

the surface alone. The statue has painted flesh but no heart, no guts. Still it's a body, nonetheless. That's our goodness, Martin."

"The body is our goodness?"

"Perfect. You're learning. My time may not be wasted. Yes, the joy of being human is living in a body. It's fine to have a body as an emblem of religion, even if it is a dead one. Do you eat meat, Martin?"

"Sometimes."

"Dead meat?"

"Of course."

"You're wrong. Meat isn't dead. You'd run a mile if offered dead meat on a plate. It would stink to high heaven. No, the meat you eat has the life of the animal still inside it. That's why it gives life to you. You think Christ rose from the dead? You're a simpleton. Christ dies and the light goes out of the universe, the big bang gets sucked back in a big whimper. Christ never died. He picked up his body and took it for a stroll. The Romans had one agenda, and he had his own. He had work still to do. There's some work you can't do outside of a body. If people could just get a hint of that, they'd thrill to being alive."

We reach the steps that lead up to my house and he trots up them, as though leading me to his own home. The door is unlocked. He kicks off his shoes in the entryway and steps inside.

"Welcome," he says, and spreads his arms wide to hug me as I step inside to join him. The hug squeezes my arms to my sides and leaves me breathless. He holds me longer than is right. It feels like he is taking an impression of my body into the flesh of his own.

"You know me?"

I shake my head.

"But you do. You know me as well as I know you. I come like this, like this storm in your life, but it is necessary. I blow in, I make things fresh and clear for you, then I blow out again. Things can grow after a storm like the one I bring. You need new growth, yes, Martin?"

I'm too numb to nod my head, so I just stare at him.

"It is so. You were dead, and now you are alive. You have many years ahead of you. Me, I have this short reprieve. Just a brief while longer to jump around in my own body. I share what I can with you before I go. And now I give you what makes my body still work as it does. I give you my name."

He holds out his hand. I take it in mine and we shake.

"Carlos," he says. "Carlos Castaneda."

. . .

There was a power in the handshake, like a whiteout that left my mind blank. I don't know how it worked. I can only say I felt more drained than charged as a result.

"*The* Carlos Castaneda?" I ask at last.

He grins, lifts his hands in the air, and spins around on his right foot before clicking his heels at a standstill again to present himself.

"But you can't be."

"Why not? I'm a writer. You're a writer. We both find our-selves in this ancient French village. It's natural that we should meet."

"But you're dead."

The smile goes from his face and he flashes into anger. "Who told you so?"

"It was reported. I read your obituary. Your body was burned and the ashes spread over the Arizona desert."

"Details," he says. "Mere details." He steps further into the room and slumps into one of the armchairs.

"They kept your death secret for a time."

"Why a time? Why not forever?"

"Your son—"

"I have no son."

"Stepson then. Your wife's son. He got an attorney's letter and released the news."

He says nothing. Simply leans back his head, opens his mouth, and lets out a long sound. It's a moan first of all, then the vocal cords stop vibrating and the sound is different. It's a death rattle. I step closer to examine him. Saliva drools from a corner of his mouth and his pupils have rolled back behind his eyelids to leave only the whites of the eyes and the veins.

There is silence, then his tongue sticks out, pink rather than gray, and remarkably juicy. It starts at the corner of his mouth and licks all the way round his lips. As I watch the tongue I feel myself watched in return. The right eyeball has swiveled back into place. One eye fixed on me, the other still white, it's like a hideous wink.

Then both eyes shut tight, stay closed awhile, and snap open. He stares up at me, opens wide his mouth, and laughs. It's a honking laugh, which seems to stem from spasms in his chest, and I feel the gusts of stale breath against my face.

I sit on the sofa to face him, with the window behind me, and wait for an explanation.

"So, dear boy." As he speaks he shifts his body to sit upright. "You think that death is the end?"

"No."

"Of course not. But look at you. See how much work you still have to do. It seems even *my* death freaks you out.

Makes you too stupid to speak. How are you going to cope with your own death when it comes?"

"Did you really die?"

"That's good. It's good you can ask the question. It means you can accept the possibility that I'll say yes. Well, poor Martin, that is my answer. Yes. Yes, Carlos Castaneda did die."

"So you're not him?"

"If I'm not, then who am I?"

"You tell me."

"OK. Let's stop playing games. You're locked inside a temporal frame, closed into your own worldview, so I will answer in your own language. I'll use a tense you can understand. I was Carlos Castaneda."

"And now?"

"A good question. Thank you for asking. As we speak I see how helpful speaking is. I've been roaming these mountains, frankly astonished to still be alive. Christ walked on water, but it seems much more miraculous for me to be walking on earth. I was sick. Sick for a long while. Cancer is interesting, experiencing your own body's decomposition while still fully conscious, but it tires you out. By the time death comes it's a relief to let go. I wasn't finished though, Martin. The Romans kept to their time schedule when they crucified Christ. He went along with it, but still had his own agenda to complete. He came back, picked up his body, and carried on. As with the Romans for him, so with cancer for me. I let it have its say. Now I'm back. It's a delight to be free of it."

"How did you manage it?" This is the magic of logic. Even when something is palpably insane, like conversing with a dead writer who's strolled into your home, logic has a structure that can keep a conversation going. "Christ's body was smothered in oils, wrapped in cloth, and laid in a tomb. You were cremated. There was nothing left but dust."

"You are asking me to justify my existence?"

"Tell me how a man can compose himself out of dust."

"You know this already. You know how a human body is formed from the matter of combusted stars."

"That's physics. We're talking metaphysics."

"I'll tell you why I'm back. The cause before the effect. Does that make sense?"

"And then you'll tell me the effect? You'll tell me how you did it?"

"If you can't work it out for yourself."

"OK," I agree.

"You have any drink in this house?"

"Wine. Beer. Whisky."

"Whisky!" The thought cheers him. "Straight up. No ice. As it comes."

I pour one for him, then one for myself—which I water down. He holds the tumbler near his nose, sniffs, and smiles. The vaporous smell of it seems enough for now. He doesn't drink.

"So," he says. "My story. Because it bores me, because it is everything I wish to escape, I will be brief. Pay attention. This bears no repetition."

CASTANEDA'S
TALE

"I was born long ago, and given the name Carlos. A fine name, and I was a fine boy, but born too close to the jungle. Most boys of an adventuring kind get to imagine a jungle. It's a place of power and myth. I got to live in one. No great inventions will ever come out of the jungle, no masterpieces of world art. A jungle is both a terrifying and an exhilarating place to grow up, for however vivid a person's mind, nature will always outstrip his imagination. A jungle forms its own sky from a canopy of leaves, gathers its own rain, teems with outlandish forms of life, sings and chants and sprouts through the day and the night. It's like living in a constant wet dream, pulsating, sticky, hot, moist, and frantic with images.

"I leave the jungle, head for Europe, later claim a home in the desert lands of the American Southwest, and I never see the boy Carlos again. What is born in the jungle can never leave. I took the shell of my adult body out to meet the best of Western civilization, but the shell was empty. I stood before the dry achievements of the world's greatest artists and architects, I read the fruits of centuries of writers and thinkers, and I was dazed. I cannot miss the boy Carlos, for even the part of me that is capable of missing him was left behind in the jungle. I was a desiccated man left to stuff his hollow body with a desiccated culture.

"People asked if my teacher Don Juan really existed. Of course he did. How could I have woken up without him? A sprinkling of datura, a dash of peyote, a swill of water, and traces of the jungle were back in my system. The sap rose within me once again.

"Others say my books are filled with invention. The dunderheads. They are blind to their own civilization and they dare to question mine? I move my life to their arid deserts so that my imagination has space to work, to recapture the essence of a truer life in words that entertain them, then they dare to use imagination as a dirty word? I spit on them. What are all the books filled with that they revere so much? Imagination. The people they vaunt as geniuses clawed through the dust of words to come up with something they think is profound. A something, now mark you this, they have maybe glimpsed yet never known as the fabric of their own lives. What I give people is not invention. It's the very essence, the energy of the boy Carlos's life.

"I do my best to stay invisible. Why do I do this? I told the world it was for fear of their capturing my spirit, binding me tight in a present moment that is soon discarded as the past. That, my man, was a lie. To get this world to understand you have to speak to it in lies. The verbal lie spared people the far greater lie of my existence. How can I go in front of people as a writer, a personality, a personage, when I know that this body they want to pay homage to is just an empty shell?

"I have ten books out in the world. They appear in many languages, in many millions of copies. Do you imagine it needs ten books to say all I have to say? Do you think it cannot all be said in this conversation between ourselves? Of course it can. Each book repeats itself, and then each book repeats the other. People thrive on repetition. They are so swamped with meaningless drivel that books are like amusement parks. There's nothing to take in but they come along for the ride. I figure if I keep writing they'll take the ride for longer. Who knows, if I keep their attention for long enough they might catch sight of the reality behind all those words.

"What is that reality? I call it a Separate Reality, but that of course is another of my lies. Reality is reality, and it's our book-reading society that is separate from it.

"Then I am dying, and I realize I am a fool. I have kept myself out of the public eye, but I forgot about the public imagination. Millions on millions of people know my name, and they each have an impression of me. For some I am like a god, for others a charlatan, it makes no difference. There is this gargantuan figure out there, a being called Carlos Castaneda, who is far from imaginary. He finds his source in my life and work, and is fed by the energy of hordes.

"My life was passing and I screamed and cursed. People said it was the pain of cancer, but they are fools. I saw the terror of my life force being tethered forever to this puffed-up, pain-filled ghost. I die, but the distorted Castaneda of people's imaginations will live on and drag me with it. To live in the public imagination, Martin, believe me that is damnation. It is fire and brimstone. Of course I screamed and cursed.

"And so I have come back. How I did so, as agreed, we leave till later. Why is very simple. I have two tasks. One, to reclaim the boy Carlos as part of myself and so be free to leave this world behind. The other, to somehow deflate the public image of me and replace it with something I can bring myself to live with. Or die with."

He chuckles, sniffs the whisky one more time, then downs it in one gulp. His eyes shine as he holds the glass out for more.

・　・　・

I take his glass, carry it down the room to the kitchen area, and notice a churning hollowness inside myself. I wonder at this effect his story has had on my system. Then I realize that meeting him has skipped me past my regular dinner hour, and the feeling is simply one of hunger.

"Would you like to eat with me?" I ask.

"What are you having?"

"Trout. I bought two in town today."

"Very good." He slaps his hands against his thighs and beams at me. "Thank you."

I prepare the trout, set the heads and tails aside for the neighborhood cat when she comes on her nightly visit, and set the fish frying with some butter and garlic and a scattering of mushrooms. I slice two potatoes thin so they will boil fast. Carlos comes and stands beside me, looking out of the kitchen window.

"Look!" he says. He sounds astonished, then breaks into laughter. From the kitchen window you can look straight down at the bend in the river some thirty feet below. This is what has amused him.

"Six," he calls out, though I am standing beside him and there is no need for such volume. "No, seven. Eight. Let me tell you, there are ten of them down there. Ten big, fat trout. You can see them from your kitchen, yet you trudge into town and pay good money for those two scrawny little things at the market."

"I was going to eat them both," I say in my own defense. "I wasn't expecting to share."

"Oh, that's fine. Don't worry about me. I haven't eaten for weeks in fact. Whatever little you can spare will amuse my stomach enough. I just wonder why you make life so difficult for yourself instead of taking what nature offers you."

"I don't know how to fish. Besides, I don't have a license."

"Is it the angler who needs the license, or the fishing tackle? Tonight we will enjoy the fruits of your voyage into town. It will be fine. And tomorrow, I shall cook for you."

He pours himself a fresh whisky and takes it back to his armchair. I concentrate on the fish, turning it over, reflecting on this new information that Carlos Castaneda seems to have come to stay. At least for one more day.

It is good to eat at last, to satisfy my stomach even while the rest of me subsides into confusion.

• • •

Carlos dabs his lips with a napkin.

"My first meal since coming alive again," he announces, looking down at his clean plate with some pride. Even the bones are chewed and swallowed.

"What have you been eating, then?"

"The sun. Like the plants, I've been feeding off the sun."

"That's why you were so hungry."

"Not at all. You are why I am so hungry. On the mountain it was enough to be part of nature, drinking occasionally from a spring. Coming down to talk with you, it brings me back to earth. Till now I have borrowed some of your energy. Thank you for it. I'll return it before I go. Now your meal has given me some energy of my own. We can both relax a little. We will get through."

"Get through what?"

"Our stories."

"I have no stories."

"A writer with no stories? You're kidding me. I know you. You have stories to tell that you don't even understand yourself yet. That's why I am here."

"To help me understand my own stories?"

"To release your stories so that we can both understand them. Your stories, I hope, hold the key that will unlock the door to my boy Carlos. My listening, I trust, will clear a path in your life in return."

"You're going to listen to my stories?"

He laughs. "You forget, dear friend, that listening is exactly what I do. My books are composed of stories I listened to. My skill is in making those stories make sense. Sense, at least, to me. So tell me, Martin. Recount your adventures in Peru."

"How do you know I was there?"

"As I was dying I returned to the country of my birth."

"Brazil?"

"That is one fact on record about my birth. A life has many births. For now, when I speak about the country of my birth, I mean Peru. I returned in energy to the country of my birth as I lay dying in Los Angeles. There I hear my name called. It is part of a conversation. And who is taking part in this conversation? Yourself. Remember it."

I hear a command, not a question. As I concentrate, the conversation slips back into my mind.

"In Cuzco?" I ask him.

He nods.

"But that was nothing. A passing reference."

"What you call a passing reference was a slander that breathed foulness on my life, but no matter. I was simply intrigued. You spoke my name, I took my chance. My name breathed out of your body, and with your next breath you took my essence in. I reached you in the highlands of Peru. You took me into the Amazonian jungle. That is my secret. That is why I have come. We will take that journey together. But first, please set the scene. Recall that conversation to get us started."

"It wasn't a conversation. At least not about you. More like an anecdote with your name slipped in. It really was nothing."

"You are forgetting two things. One is that I am asking you to tell me what I already know. That's OK. You'll learn to accept that in time. The second thing you are forgetting is less forgivable."

He closes his mouth, clamping hold of the silence.

"What's that?" I'm eventually forced to ask. "What's the second thing?"

"You dare to ask me that, when I know words are wasted on you?"

"How do you mean, words are wasted on me?"

"Martin!" He snaps my name out, calling me to attention. "What's one of the first things you learned in the ceremony last September?"

"How do you know about the ceremony? Nobody knows about that."

"How? Another question? Why bother with your questions, when you refuse to learn what you've already been shown? Last September, what did you learn about words? Tell me."

His attitude throws me. I'm so stunned by what he apparently knows about me that I forget what I know about myself and have no answer for him at first. He sits with his arms locked in position against his knees, his body motionless, and stares at me. I close my eyes to escape from him for a moment. It gives me a chance to collect myself, to step back into that room in New Mexico of almost a year before and bring it back into my mind.

THE FIRST
AYAHUASCA
JOURNEY

The room was a large one in an old adobe compound, cleared of furniture so all the participants had space to lie on the wooden floor. The Peruvian shaman called the circle's attention to the ritual that would begin our second ceremony. My life was about to change.

Maybe not as much as it's changing now though, with Carlos in the room. I let my narration dwindle into silence. Well, not silence, but the series of highly vocal yawns Carlos is emitting.

"Don't mind me," he assures me. "I'm simply yawning to keep myself alive."

"Alive?"

"You bet. You know what I gave my life to? The power of myth. I am one of the greatest storytellers this century has known. Yet as I sit here listening to you drone on, I come to see a fatal flaw in all I ever wrote. It was fine at the time, but it's old-fashioned now. Have you ever done any guided meditations?"

"A few."

"And how did they start? You were sitting by a pool in a forest. You heard a sound . . . ?"

"Something like that."

"Nothing like that. You ARE sitting by a pool . . . You HEAR a sound. Present tense, not past. Everything is now. As you tell your story, don't confine it to the past. Don't kill it off. Take me there so I'm living it with you. I'm alive now because I'm living life with you. Don't kill me off with your choice of tense. That's too funny a way for a writer to expire."

I carry on, and try to make the shift he's looking for.

Attending the ceremony is a breakthrough in itself. Having enjoyed transformative visionary experiences without taking any form of psychedelic medicine, I am unsure of surrendering myself to their powers. One name has attracted me, however. *Ayahuasca.* I heard the name, and it resounded in me like a call. When I was a young boy the jungles of the Amazon were my dream destination. Now ayahuasca comes out of the Amazon as an emissary. First the name, and then the plant medicine itself.

I like the term "plant medicine" instead of "drug." I am intrigued to hear of the "teachings" ayahuasca has to offer. Pleased too that it comes out of an ancient native tradition, and that a shaman steeped in the ways of the jungle is bringing the medicine to us. I kneel in front of him, take the tiny vessel in my hands, and tip the bitter liquid down my throat.

Carlos interrupts me.

"Goodbye," he says, stands up, and walks to the door.

"What's wrong?"

He steps outside. I go out to find him standing by the wall, looking down the valley.

"You're bored with your own story. If that's your mood, I'm wasting my time. You'll never write the book I need you to write."

"I'm not bored. I'm just getting started."

"Tiny!" Spittle flies from his mouth as he utters the word. "A tiny cup. A bitter liquid. A Peruvian shaman. Throw in an adjective and be done with it. You're like the rest of them. Stuck on being a famous living writer, and you haven't even started living."

"It's you that died."

"I lived first. You know how I lived? I gave my attention to everything around me. You know what paying attention does? It makes you God! It's the power of creation, the power to give life. Fail to notice something, and it's no longer there. It fades from existence. Be a man. Find the quality in what surrounds you. Then you'll see how reciprocal life is. Then you'll no longer be half-dead, for the qualities in you will come to life. Be that kind of man, then be a writer."

He goes quiet.

"Life is in the details," he adds.

The silence hangs a while longer.

"The cup is made of clay," I try. "Light to the touch. And warm somehow. Like cupping a bird in your hands. Slighter than you could believe, seeming vulnerable, yet with a life inside that beats in a way I don't know how. This cup is brown, but with an intricate design in white around its topmost half that's like a maze. Just holding this cup is like going on a journey."

Carlos looks at me.

"Maybe," he says. "You think you can keep it up?"

"I'll try."

"Storytellers have the power of life and death. You'd better try hard."

He turns from me, walks back into the house, and sits back down in the armchair. I follow. I close my eyes to picture the space first, check around the New Mexican room for all the details, see what interests me as I revisit that time, then resume the story.

. . .

Ayahuasca comes from the stem of a vine, thicker than a man's wrist and brown and gnarled as a tree trunk. Hammered into pulp, mixed with *chicruna* leaves to render its powers active, it is brewed into a brown potion that is quaintly called tea.

I take little notice of the shaman while we are all choosing our spot to lie on the floor, assembling our little range of possessions: our mat, our pillow, our blankets, our water, our bowl should we need to be sick. A slight man, his nose beaked, graying hair that skirts his shoulders, floral shirt, drawstring trousers, skin tanned and leathered beyond his middle age, the shaman is a fairly typical Santa Fe type. At first I presume he is one of the evening's participants. Then a robe dropped over his head transforms him. It is a pale robe, reaching to his knees, its design in simple brown ink an expanse of the mazelike pattern drawn around the ceremonial cup. My eyes seek to travel different routes through the maze. It makes me dizzy, so I let my eyesight blur.

A wind blows. I hear it, a thin and rhythmical wind, then realize it is a near-whistle of a chant being blown across the top of the liquid. The shaman is singing his power into the medicine. A light flares in the darkening room, the tobacco glows in the bowl of his pipe, he blows smoke across the surface of the liquid, and the ayahuasca is wakened to its powers.

I swallow my dose at sunset, but the room has already drawn itself back into shadows as clouds swarm through the sky. Rains thrash the windows behind the shaman's back, a lightning flash and a roar of thunder energize the room. The medicine is bitter. I lie down to wait for it to take effect.

"Words . . . ," I say to Carlos. I'm nervous about losing his attention again. "I know you asked me about words, but can I speak about sound first?"

He nods.

The medicine is a psychedelic, so I expect visions, but it is my hearing that hallucinates first. It opens, it broadens, until I am no longer listening from inside the limits of my body. The scope of my listening changes. I hear the soft breathing of a person at the far end of the room, but the breathing seems so close to my ear it is as loud as a wind. Another person moves a limb, and the crack of that person's bones sounds in my own joints. On a bare wooden floor, in a house set in the desert, I hear rustlings in the undergrowth. Without looking, with my eyes closed in the gathering darkness, I recognize a mouse that is nuzzling through leaves near my head. It is the same mouse I killed in a trap that afternoon, thinking my trailer home was too small for both the creature and myself. As I hear it pattering across the floor, the tiny sounds thud into my flesh.

This is the way a jungle floor hears things. I have become the ears of the jungle.

My body stretches. Rolling from my mat to the hardness of the floor, my body luxuriates in pushing out its limbs. There are no aches, there is no tension.

"Sounds as good as death," Carlos comments.

"Do you ache now?"

"Everything is relative." He adjusts his body in the armchair. "Death was good though."

This time with ayahuasca is good too. Every position my body discovers finds it nestling in comfort. I begin to see the magic in this first lesson from ayahuasca. The bounds of my self-perception alter. From being tethered to a human body, my experience expands to take me back to the source of the medicine. I become a jungle vine.

"Show me!" Carlos sits forward in his chair to watch.

"Show you what?"

"I want to observe you as a jungle vine."

"It's a story. In the past. I was on a drug high. I can't just do it."

"Of course you can. Ayahuasca showed you the way. You can go back anytime. You should know that, but of course you don't. We'll come back to it later. Do you remember earlier times when you morphed into something else?"

I think awhile, but come up with nothing.

"No memories of swings? Kicking out and sailing high, your little body at one with the swing and the motion and the surging to new heights? Funny, I was sure I recalled something like that in your past. Never mind. Your story's not bad. I'm staying alive for it. Go on."

One member of the group keeps taking a drink of water. I hear it pour down his throat and trickle through his body. It seems an exaggerated thirst until I recognize a truth that surprises me. This man is not drinking for himself. Someone else in the room is thirsty. His drinking quenches that other person's thirst.

While this is happening a monologue chatters on inside my head. I praise myself for all that is happening to me. As ayahuasca pushes me on into new realms of experience I pity those still stuck in my old view of life. I compare myself to my friends, to my partner, and find countless points of niggling grievance in our relationships. And as this inner monologue mutters on, the teachings of ayahuasca keep interrupting me. It has no wisdom that it can offer me on my own, for if it does so that wisdom will become poisonous. I am so stuck on the need to think myself special, so fixed on the notion that my life is defined in competition with others, that I have to get rid of this fatal flaw in my nature before any progress can be made. I have to get rid of the idea that I am separate and acknowledge that I am a part of all things. Ayahuasca does not want to warp me any further by inflating my ego. It needs me to see that there is no benefit for anybody that is not also a universal benefit.

As my center of hearing expands through the acreage of jungle floor, as I recognize that one person can quench another person's thirst in the way that you water roots to give strength to leaves, my limited concepts of myself loosen. I had heard the spiritual truth that "we are one another," without learning how to live the fact. Now the fact becomes part of my living experience. It becomes undeniable.

. . .

"Ha!"

The noise from Carlos startles me. He relaxes his posture and slumps back in his chair as though someone has punched him in the solar plexus.

"What's up?"

"Undeniable, you say?"

Carlos sticks his fingers down his throat and pretends to vomit. I watch him gagging, expect to see his trout come swimming up to splash on the stone floor. Then he stops and looks at me.

"I'm waiting for you to come up with the truth about words, and you spew up stuff like that. Should I simply despair of you? The lesson you've learned is undeniable, is it? One gulp of a magic potion, the first hour of the first psychedelic trip of your life, and you've already vanquished the ego?

"I tell you this, though I don't know why I bother because you listen to nothing. But I tell you this one truth in any case. Nothing in a man's life is undeniable. We have endless, boundless, limitless capacities to fool ourselves. Look at Peter, the first saint and model among men, forewarned by Jesus Christ himself, yet when the cock crows three times he sees that man's capacity to deny anything has blossomed in himself. And do you know what? I bet even Peter didn't learn his lesson. Fall once, and you have it in you to fall again."

"That was his lesson?"

"That's your lesson. Peter's was of a different order. I don't know if he learned it or not. I came back to life before the two of us could discuss the matter. When the rooster crowed thrice, when Peter denied Christ, do you think it mattered to Jesus? Of course it didn't. Jesus was busy with his own troubles. In denying he knew Jesus, Peter was denying the Christ in himself. He identified with his body and denied his soul. What was his lesson? To wake up to himself whenever he hears a rooster crow. Nature's more reliable than our minds. It keeps in constant harmony with creation. I like to use birdsong that way. Hear a bird sing, and I pause to recollect who I am.

"But what do you want with Peter's lesson? You don't remember your own. That's why I had to put on this old body to be here with you now. Otherwise we'd be having this exchange on some other level, and I'd be free. Instead of that, I'm here to interrupt you. 'We are one another,' you say. Go on."

"Am I wrong in thinking that?"

"Think what you like, it doesn't bother me. I just question the degree to which you learned it."

His voice is calm now, his body relaxed.

"Besides, I was bored. You were getting lost in the story. Entranced by the flow of your own words. I stopped you before you zoomed on past the point we're looking for. Words are escape valves. Passions, pressures, boredom, madness, shame, they all take flight that way. Words mesmerize us like lullabies and goad us like war chants. They guide us through the dull mechanics of life. Yet there is still a truth in words. You saw it when you let go of your sense of self and recognized a group as a whole composed of elements such as yourself. At this point in your story, if not in your life, you see this. So carry on. Tell me the truth of words."

And I remember.

"Words came back to me," I say. "Snatches of conversation. Pieces of good advice. I didn't pay much attention to them at the time. Now I saw the mistake in that."

"What sort of advice?"

I look for an example, and smile at the first that comes into my head.

"It sounds silly now."

"Try me."

"It was a sentence spoken by a lifeguard I met on the beach at Carpinteria, about ninety miles north of LA."

"I know the place well."

"She wasn't a friend or anything. I only met her that once, a quick interview for a *Baywatch*-flavored magazine piece I was writing. The sentence was her advice for any youngster starting out on a lifeguarding career. 'Always use the best sunscreen,' she said. 'Never go the cheap route.'"

"And that advice seems silly to you?"

"Not silly. Just not very consequential."

"Go back. Close your eyes as you did before. Review the setting. Tell me what was happening when you heard this sentence again."

I do as he asks. Go back in my imagination to the room and the ceremony. Recall the sensation of surrendering control of my body. This is nothing to do with torpor or inertness. Nothing to do with trembling or fits. It is simply and wondrously accepting that a will beyond my own has control of my movements. It needs no decision of mine for me to move or be still. My body recognizes when an action suits it, and responds accordingly.

• • •

My body sits up and I watch two participants, a man and a woman, stand and move around the room. They stoop a little as they move, their outlines smudged and gray in the darkness. The sight washes me clean of millennia of conditioning. My view of myself as a human being is stripped away as an ancestral memory takes its place. The man and woman appear as figures from the Stone Age, cave dwellers after dusk at a time before our myths have been reduced into words.

My body rises, not of my volition but stirred by some other prompting, and goes to join them.

They prepare a second dose of ayahuasca for themselves. My hands reach out to the man, an apprentice to the shaman, and receive a fresh bowl of the medicine. It is weightless and floats toward my face. Before bringing it to my lips, I look into it. The tiny vessel disappears from sight and the tea takes on the appearance of a knot in a dark piece of wood, a spiraled whorl cupped in my hand. Looking into this whorl is a journey in itself, for the whorl stretches out in the form of a long tunnel. It is a journey into the essence of the ayahuasca. I fall in love with its look and its color.

Then my head rises, and the bowl touches my lower lip. I smell it as it rests there, and wait for the medicine to give itself to me. The bowl waits for its moment, then tips its contents into my mouth.

Ayahuasca feeds itself to me. I know it is this way, rather than anything so simple as my taking a drink. Ayahuasca is inside me, it has already taken over my limbs as though they are outreaches of a vine, and then sent my body out to receive this extra potion. Now is a moment of initiation. My mouth holds the liquid for a while, moving it round to flow against every atom of my palate, and then one swallow and the medicine pours down inside me.

Back on my mat, I sit while my right hand reaches up. Its fingers stroke my cheek, feeling the dryness of the skin. I feel sad that I am taking such little care of this body that is in my charge. It is being ravaged by my summer treks in deserts and mountains, by living at the high New Mexican altitude. It is then that the sentence comes to me, the advice on sunscreen from a lifeguard met once on a Californian beach.

. . .

"Now it's August," Carlos observes. "I met you when you were coming back from a walk in these French mountains. The thunderstorm broke what has been a very hot time. Tell me, are you wearing sunscreen, quality or otherwise?"

"I've got some with me."

He laughs. "Touch the skin on your face."

"It's dry," I admit after doing so. "Flaky."

"What a figure you are. What an example of denial. You're given a lesson from an expert on skin care, it's repeated as part of a sacred rite, a reminder stares you in the face whenever you look in a mirror, you accept the need to apply the lesson in your life, yet still you deny it. You think your body's inconsequential? Then you deserve to go through the mill of retrieving it from the dust of death.

"You're a human being who doesn't value his body. A writer who doesn't value words. You're a sorry case, Martin. "

"I do value words."

"You value their sound, their form, their texture, their flow. You're into the aesthetic of words. But you're the same as everyone else in these benighted times. In olden days, in what we so pitifully term the Dark Ages, sorcerers could reckon with the power of words. They were mighty things. Now they are simply pearls before swine.

"And here too am I, beyond the silence of the grave, talking too much."

He stops speaking. I feel the silence grow too heavy.

"I did learn a lesson," I say. "I just forget to apply it."

"Ha!"

"At night, before sleeping, I rerun all the conversations of the day. At least I mean to. And not just conversations, chance remarks overheard in passing too. I look for any resonance. Anything that seems to carry some special meaning."

"And then?"

"I fall asleep."

He chuckles. I smile back.

"You exasperate me," he says. "But I'm glad I've come. There's a lot you have to be shown. You've found the resonance. The vibration. That's good. Isolate that quality and you have a chance of sifting the words of truth from the garbage.

"Words are energy, Martin. You will never know how much this universe calls for us to act in harmony with it, how it yearns for us to remove the blinkers of separation. Like a gulf stream squeezed inside the oceans, it is an energy that calls us to our senses. It runs a message through the drivel of our lives. It pours itself through people's heads, in one ear and out the other, and finds voice now and again in the tenor of their words. Make our restless selves still for a while, tune ourselves to that energy, and more of such words will spill from our mouths.

"Loudspeakers don't show musical mastery in transmitting the works of Bach. We don't show wisdom in speaking inspired words. Pay attention to our own speech, however, and we develop our powers of listening.

"It's only in listening that truth can be heard. In listening to our own words or the words of others, stay alert for the resonance. Even clichés take fire when we truly hear them for the first time. Tell me, Martin, do you think that animals lie, any more than flowers or trees or rivers lie?"

I give it some thought. "I suppose not."

"You're right. Lying is a quality unique to humans. There are no lies outside of the human condition, as there is no truth. There is harmony but there is no truth. Nobody ever speaks the truth, for as words are spoken they are still unheard. Truth is born in the act of deep listening, not of speaking, when words find resonance in a person's being. What do you think happens to that truth?"

I'm barely following the sense of this. "I don't know," I admit.

"It nearly always expires. It shimmers and fades through lack of attention, and suddenly it's gone. Truth when heard doesn't enter the fabric of our world until someone bothers to apply it. People must give awareness to what they hear and then act on it.

"Think, tonight, if what I say is true. From the look on your face, I can tell that no truth has registered yet. See if the echo of my words has a resonance. Then, application or denial, the choice is yours."

He looks above my head, out at the darkening sky.

"Would you like to go outside for a while?" I ask. "I normally like to sit out there at dusk."

"You've not recalled your use of my name in Peru yet."

"No," I admit, but I stand up to lead the way outdoors in any case. Sometimes two writers can be too much of a load for one room. I need to get some air.

4

THE KINGDOM
OF THE INCAS

I call the cat Maxine, as though she's my pet. In fact it's me that belongs to her. I moved into her territory and she trained me to deliver scraps of food. Other householders in her territory offer her the same service.

The ring of porcelain against stone, as the plate of fish trimmings hits the ledge, is her call. She scampers down the steps and leaps up to the wall to bite at her dinner. Splotched in patches of black, brown, and white, this mottled cat has torn ears and scars around her brow. Her belly is heavy with one of her semiannual broods. Twice a year she disappears to some hole in the hillside, to drop and possibly eat her litter, then reappears on the rounds of her territory.

I tell Carlos nothing of this. We simply watch her eat, clean her paws, and pace away. Maxine is her own world of mystery. We have ours.

We sit on chairs and face the hillsides. Bats explode from the buildings behind us to flutter mere inches from our faces. They then stream down to catch insects above the river some way below. Sitting side by side we let the daylight fade. The first stars appear before I break the silence.

"Peru was my first time in the southern hemisphere," I tell him. "I was excited about seeing a totally different night-time sky. Eager to see the Southern Cross. Then there it was, a constellation as simple and unspectacular as a kite, pinned against a largely empty sky. I saw how silly I was, to want to see the southern skies when the starscape above my own country is so dense and rich I can never hope to fathom it."

"People say 'live in the moment,'" Carlos responds. "They think it's truth but it's only hindsight. If it were the truth they wouldn't need to state it, they'd be living it. Knowing what we've got before it's gone, that's the secret of life. You're lucky. You had a chance to miss your northern skies while you were still able to come back and appreciate them. I'm lucky too. I missed being in a body, and here I am."

"You talk about truth not existing till it's heard," I recollect. This is a new idea, so I pause to think it through. It's good that we're both looking out in the same direction, so I don't have to face him as I carry on. "So it's not true that you've come back from the dead. There's only me to hear it, and I don't believe it. So if that's not true, what's the point in us talking? Whatever we say will be based on a lie."

"You're not the only one here." He stays quiet while I wonder what he means. "I'm here."

I look aside at him. He sits very trimly on the wooden seat, smiling, his back straight, his face angled toward the sky.

"My own words resonate in me," he continues. "It's quite thrilling."

"You don't care that I don't believe you?"

"But you do. You're merely in denial. The way you denied me in Peru even before we'd met."

So I recall and recount the story he wants to hear. It seems so insignificant, so paltry a thing, yet it is obviously going to keep coming up in our conversation till I have got it out of the way.

. . .

"It was just a dinner-table conversation."

"Pathetic."

I look across as Carlos turns his chair around to face me.

"You're a professional storyteller, yet you start off a tale with two of the biggest mistakes in the book. That word 'just,' apologizing before you start out, as though your story isn't worth listening to. Any story's worth listening to if you make it worth the telling. And what about setting the scene? Who's there? Where's this dinner table? A second failing in only one sentence, a story without context. I want the sights, the smells, the sounds. I'm hungry for this scene. So give it me."

"Give me time."

"No. My attention's wandering. You've got to grab it. You can even charge your silences with meaning if you make the storytelling effort. So try."

I take a deep breath as he rattles his chair around to face the stars once again. I'm tempted to say forget it, this is my house and I'm going to bed. Please go so I can lock the door behind you and sleep safely. But of course I don't, for although this is my house it isn't my story anymore. Carlos is reeling it out of me. So while he's sitting there, playing the line as the river runs below him, angling for a bigger and better story, I find I have to carry on.

. . .

The time is dusk, darkness swooping down above the main square of Cuzco. It is an ancient city built by the Incas to be their stronghold, the place where their kings and sorcerer-priests maintained the esoteric knowledge on which their empire was built. The plan of the city takes the form of the fabled jaguar. Following the folds of green hills in this high Andean valley, the head of this jaguar is in the great stone compound of Sacsayhuaman some way above us. Here in this ancient square of Cuzco, we are somewhere near the heart.

(I admit to hamming up the story, childishly goaded by Carlos's criticism. However he doesn't rise to the bait. Instead he looks rapt. I continue in the same mode, setting aside my regular literary taste, until I find I am actually enjoying myself.)

Our party is housed in a building that fronts the square. The building takes paying guests, and though this makes it a hotel such status is only a concession to modern times. Tourists arrive in little buses, throng the alleys and streets, little knowing that they are in fact the ghosts and that the spirits and figures of earlier times still teem and swirl around them. Cuzco was built to survive earthquakes, to endure through millennia, not for the sake of tourists or the small concerns of modern-day merchants. It is the heart of the Incan empire, and the heart is still beating. Someday, when Earth can bear the sight of such magnificence as the Incas now hide from our view, the glories of that empire may be revealed again. And the hotel where we are staying will drop all pretenses and once again exude the power of its days as a temple building, the palatial home of the virgins of the Sun God. Maidens selected and cherished for their beauty led brief and pampered lives here, before their purity was offered up in sacrifice to the heavens.

The walls of my room are composed of gray polygonal stones, cut to sit snug against each other without the ephemeral smearing of mortar. Trapezoidal niches sit high in the walls, waiting for incense and idols to be returned to them. The toilet that is set in front of the sealed doorway will be smashed as figures resume their bodily substance and demand right of passage through the bathroom.

Stirred by hunger, two of us step out and dart between the shadows of peddlers still hawking wares in the square as daylight fades. We head past the Spanish cathedral on our right-hand side and aim for lights in the nearest café, set inside the galleried walkway that fronts most of these buildings. A waiter shows us to a table near the window, with no cloth covering, so that the dark varnished oak of its surface reflects the café's strips of naked neon lights.

Music soothes us, comfortingly familiar, the clear single notes of a piano stilling the air and summoning the orchestra for the slow movement of Beethoven's third piano concerto. Behind the sound, more subtle but thrilling too, is the sizzle of onions in a pan. Their smell mingles with the aroma of newly baked bread. The waiter takes our order for cheese omelettes and we relax into the sense of having discovered our Peruvian home-away-from-home.

It is then that the tiny figure of don Pedro steps in through the door. His beaked nose seems to have drawn him in, on the trail of an evening snack. He looks our way, catches my eye, and I nod and gesture toward the spare seat at our table. We're pleased to see him. This is the shaman accompanying our party, and no one yet seems to have spent private time with him. Or at least if they did they aren't telling, as we might tell no one about this meeting of ours.

"The doors of the cathedral were open next door," he announces once he has settled down and ordered the same meal as we. "A mass was about to begin. I could see the candles glowing. It was decision time. Food for the soul, or food for the body. So I veered left, and here I am."

"Do shamans go to church?" I ask.

"I have known several shamans who became Christian." He nibbles at a slice of bread. Though he seems to be eating hungrily, half the feeble slice will still be left at the end of his meal. "They last for two, three, maybe five years. Then they have to give it up and become shamans again. Christianity is all about love. They cannot abide so much love."

"What's shamanism about then, if it's not about love?"

He simply looks at me and raises one eyebrow.

I've asked the question. Now it's for me to find my own answer. It will be one of the fiercest challenges of the coming months.

. . .

We have finished our omelettes, dabbed the juice of soft-cooked eggs from our mouths, and spoken about our itinerary while based in Cuzco, when don Pedro suddenly returns the conversation to shamanism. Now that his hunger is satisfied he is more free for matters of the soul.

"Sex," he announces. "We shamans have a high sense of our own calling, but seven times out of ten that's what shamanism is about. Few people care for the distinctions. Shaman, *curandero,* sorcerer, they have no interest in the terms. When people come to me for help only one thing is on their minds. Sex. They want more virility; they want someone's heart; they want to free themselves of one person so as to go with another. The shaman cannot say what shamanism is about. He serves the desires of others."

He stops speaking and stares across the table, sensing a challenge.

"I don't believe that."

The challenge comes from Keith, my companion at our table. He is a litigation lawyer, and I shall come to value his clear-sightedness on this trip. Though he's a native New Yorker, his Irish ancestry seems the strongest element in him—his blue eyes, pale complexion, curls of dark hair, and high-arched dancer's feet that always seem to have skipped around you so that his comments keep coming from an angle different than you expect. He speaks softly, blinks slowly, but never misses a beat.

"I wouldn't be here, don Pedro, if I didn't respect your intelligence. You can't have chosen to be a slave to the desires of others. There has to be more to your choice of profession than that."

Don Pedro smiles, recognizing our conversation has become a debate, and responds. "I'm no slave. No one receives the services of a shaman without payment of some kind. In my travels I meet very poor people who need help. 'Why don't you go to your shaman?' I ask them, and they tell me it is because they have nothing to give in exchange. If they have nothing to give, then he will take what they do not want to give him. He will take their souls. There are always forces clustered around a shaman, glad to lend him their services for the payment of a soul."

Keith is not satisfied. "You have a grander philosophy than that, don Pedro. I know you have. There's some ambition that keeps you going."

Don Pedro sucks the last of his soda up through a straw before continuing. He uses the pause to take the argument back into history.

"When the Spanish first came to the jungle they found no churches and no idols, so they said there was no religion. They found no trading posts, so they said there was no civilization. Jungles are dark and the Spaniards were blinded by the light of their own expectations, so they could not see the riches that were there.

"Hopefully it will be different for you—the invisible that is there will be made apparent. Maybe for now you are a little like those Spaniards. You think there is commerce, there is religion, there are these neat little pockets that life slips into. I tell you a shaman satisfies desires at a price and you want something more. You want a grand philosophy. In the jungle religion and commerce are all one thing. The shaman is a banker. He administers the natural powers. He goes to the guardian spirits of the animals, the rivers, the plants, the birds, the trees, and he finds out what they can spare. He pays his dues in ritual, then tells his people what is coming to them, the hunters what will be their catch and the gatherers what to gather. The shaman is the intermediary between man and the environment. When the bank is empty, when the natural resources are too depleted, no more loans can be made. He learns of this from the nature guardians, passes on the message, and his people move to a different region.

"You ask if I have an ambition. If I do, it is that. I want people to reawaken to the shaman's role of administering the forces of nature. I want to gather a group of people and an area of land and put these old shamanic ways of managing the land into practice.

"But it is a distant ambition. Here we are, away from the jungle, and remnants of a great civilization are all around us. Could the Spaniards see that when they came here? Of course not. All they saw was the gold and the religious trappings. The real power of the area was invisible. I have a friend, a humble and so a great man. For years he lived in these mountains and took down dictation of a great work, learning from plants in the way you are learning. This book is a great spiritual history of the region. Some may call it fantasy, deny that you can take dictation from vegetable matter, but for me his book is more true than any history book from any university press. My friend was trained by a great master here in Peru. He and two colleagues were the master's apprentices. One of these you probably know. He is big in the West. Wrote books about a teacher called Don Juan."

"Carlos Castaneda," I say.

"My friend's book is only in Spanish, one limited edition. Castaneda's sell in many copies and many languages everywhere in your Western world. Each civilization gets the books it deserves."

"So Castaneda studied here in Peru?" I ask. He does not answer or nod his head, but simply watches as I carry on. "You're saying your friend wrote spiritual truth and Castaneda's books are a sham? They give the West what it is looking for, not what it needs?"

Keith has danced around the conversation to add a point of his own. "The shaman caters to people's desires."

Don Pedro smiles and stands up. "These are your words, not mine. Enough talking, I think. We've an early start tomorrow. It's time for sleep. Thank you for my dinner."

He leaves me with the check, and I'm happy to pay it. There's a chance this shaman has done me some service during our conversation. I don't want to be in his debt.

. . .

"Good," Carlos declares, and slaps his knees. "You know the part I like best? When don Pedro forces you to say my name. Ha! The man is on my side! Now you have spoken at last. The story is out. But you missed an important detail."

"What was that?"

Above the sound of the river and the croaking frogs I hear him exhale, then suck the air in again.

"You speak my name"—he breathes out again—"and with your next breath you take me in. We two are one. This is it, Martin. This is where our story begins."

He stands. "We've an early start tomorrow. Time for my sleep."

Without my invitation he reenters my house and lays himself down on the sofa. Smaller than I imagined him, five feet six or so, he fits on it without the need to curl up. I follow him indoors and am about to ask him to leave when he interrupts me. His voice is gruff. I don't understand, but before I can query his comment he repeats it.

The man is on his back, his lips vibrating, and the sound I am hearing is a snore.

5

THE POWER
OF MOUNTAINS

Carlos doesn't shake me. His hand simply grips my shoulder.

I seize hold of it, push and twist, but he's firmly planted and doesn't move.

"I startled you," he says. "Were you dreaming?"

I was, but being wakened scared all the dreams from me. "What time is it?"

The bell in the church tower clangs out the first of six beats as my answer. After some debate the clock was set to match the sleeping pattern of the village mayor, staying silent after his ten o'clock bedtime and becoming active again to raise him at six. It is still pitch-black outside and far too early for me.

I turn over and go back to sleep.

"Get up, Martin!" Carlos calls before going back downstairs. "Hurry. Get your clothes on. The start of a new day is much too exciting to sleep through."

I get up. He waits for me outside, my backpack already on his back. The air outdoors is fresh but surprisingly chilly.

41

Venus still shines like a bright pin in the black sky over to the southwest.

Carlos says nothing but walks away.

"That's my backpack," I tell him.

"Don't worry. It's not heavy. We'll take turns."

And for some reason, maybe his momentum, maybe my docility, I find myself walking with him.

We go around the side of the house and up steps through alleyways lit a soft yellow by lanterns. This first passageway is the Rue des Moines, the street of the monks. Centuries ago they headed out from their monastery further south toward Spain, and walked up through the mountains till they reached this particular bend in the river and sensed they were home. My own home was once a goathouse belonging to this community of monks. Houses cluster round the hillside, their stone walls curving round to fill the available slots.

Our route leads us around the church, gargoyles peering out from its tower. The dial on the clock is brightly lit, the time just past six o'clock. As we step around the church walls to start on the track up the mountain, the bells strike again. There is no chance of missing the passage of time in this ancient village. The clock strikes each hour twice so workers on the terraces of distant hillsides can grow still and count the chimes the second time around.

Nothing stirs around the tombs of the graveyard down to our right. It's too early for the pack of hunting dogs penned to our left as well, who normally love to bark and howl at anything that passes. Too early for anything but sleep, in my humble opinion of the moment. I struggle to keep up with Carlos as he gathers speed, not running or seeming to race at all but still ascending the asphalt track at a pace that leaves me breathless.

The path winds until the terraces of old vineyards are left behind, and carries on between plantings of scrub oak. The air is scented by wild bushes of rosemary and thyme and clusters of lavender, and across to the east the sky is tinted with the first orange streak of sunrise.

"Here!" Carlos declares, and we leave the track to walk through the soft dry grass of a meadow, the silhouettes of poplars becoming clear against the lightening sky. After some twenty yards the meadow vanishes over the edge of the hill, but a cluster of weathered rocks borders the drop. Carlos climbs up, and gestures for me to come and sit beside him. The rocks are rounded and matted with lichen. It is easy to become comfortable, though not as comfortable as in my own bed.

We sit in silence for a while, Carlos looking straight ahead while I look around. The only drama seems to be that the stars are fading, and I fail to find the charm of the moment.

Carlos takes off the backpack and reaches his hand into it, looking at me to draw my attention. He's like some kiddies' magician with his hand in a top hat. I don't care if he brings out a rabbit or even a camel. I don't want to be impressed.

"Do I know you, or do I know you?" he asks. And pulls out the thermos flask from my kitchen. Like real magic he unscrews the top and pours me a mugful of hot, strong tea. With milk, without sugar. The way I like it. At last I manage to shed a smile on the day. He watches me drink.

"So now, young Martin, are miracles possible?"

"Anything's possible after my morning tea." I smile again. "Thanks."

He doesn't drink himself, but reaches into the pack to pull out something else. I recognize the black leather tubular casing of my monocular. I bought it in Berlin shortly after the Wall came down, from a market stall set up under the Brandenburg Gate. Part of old Soviet army supplies. I tried it out for the first time on the statue on top of the Gate's high archway. It was one of the visual shocks of my life. Expecting sculpture, I was looking instead down the flared nostrils of a horse that was charging toward me. I dropped the monocular for the naked-eye view, pale and distant horses pulling a chariot, then dared to look through my monocular again. The city surroundings were charged with stunning detail as I moved the lens around. I bought the monocular and carried it to France.

Carlos brings the instrument to his eye. His mouth opens, and a soft gasp follows. I look in the direction he is aiming, but notice nothing. The sky is empty of the eagles and lammergeyers I sometimes see spreading their wings up there. There is nothing but the gradual unfolding of hills and mountains toward the more distant view.

"Now put down your tea and enter the day," Carlos commands, and passes the monocular to me.

I scan the landscape, still blind to what I am seeing.

"Mont Canigou," he pronounces, and the syllables of the name seem to bring it to life. The first daylight is touching the high flanks now, the coating of their scrub and trees like green fur. And then the mountain ridge, arching from the left to dip into a deep ridge and join the rounded half-dome of the mountain's peak. This is the sacred mountain of the Pyrenees. Whether coated in snow, clear and bare like today, or shimmering in haze that makes the whole mountain some ethereal wash against the sky, Canigou is the spot on Earth that holds all the aspirations of the local Catalan people.

Magnified many times so that its details pounce against my right eye, Canigou suddenly seems as close as a companion. The rocks where Carlos and I are sitting have become broad enough to hold us all, two men and a sacred mountain. That is the sense the sight of Canigou achieves, light filtering in above the Mediterranean to turn the whole of the eastern Pyrenees into one vast yet intimate space that holds us at its center.

"You know something about sacred mountains," Carlos remarks.

I wish sometimes he would pose comments on my life as questions rather than statements. It's satisfying to have nuggets of your own life you can present from time to time as a surprise to those who think they know you. Carlos appears to draw his knowledge of me not from research, but rather from access into the center of my life.

"It seems unfair that I should know so much about your life." So now Carlos is even speaking from knowledge of my current thoughts. He's reading my mind. "But nothing is unfair. Everything comes down to exchange in the end. This is not about some mind-reading skill I've developed. I live your life as though it's my own. I have access to any moment in your history. Perhaps I live your life more consciously than you do, but that's just a qualitative difference. And where I have access to the inner workings of your life, you of course have access to mine. In time you may experience this. For now sharing your life is enough. And your experience of mountains such as these."

I once wrote a book about my travels to sacred mountains of the world. Cherry blossoms forming a pink and delicate dawn out of which Mount Fuji rises. The chills of Kilimanjaro reaching through two sleeping bags, waking me to study its beauty through my clouds of breath. The rapture of light burnishing Ayers Rock. Snow and ice wiping me clean on my pilgrimage to Kailas, my first sight of its peak being like a reinvention of my soul. For all I have studied mountains, they remain an impenetrable mystery to me.

"Mountains fascinate you," Carlos informs me. "Maybe if I tell you my understanding of them, it will help unlock the mystery of me. You already know everything I know, but until you understand that fact I'll have to reveal it to you. That's why we've come to this spot, on the dawn of this new day. We'll share what we know of mountains while we sit in front of this mighty one. It'll remind us that our words are more important than we recognize.

"You will begin. Tell me about Machu Picchu."

"I've nothing to say. I've only been there twice. No more than a week in all."

"Stop it! No more apologizing. You're a storyteller. Start with the setting."

Somehow it's harder to set a mountain than a conversation. Geographical statistics don't do it and a physical description barely comes close. We see mountains as rock, as vast and solid statements on the landscape, but when we do that we miss the story. Mountains are heaved up from the core of the earth, they are shaped by sun and wind and water. Rivers curl round their bases, streams spring from their sides, air licks and buffets them, and what we see is never solid but in a permanent state of flux. It is a living sculpture, being remodeled every moment by the forces of nature.

Carlos understands this. He allows me time to sit in silence before I begin.

· · ·

There are two ways to approach Machu Picchu: from above and from below.

The first comes after days of trekking. The Inca Trail rises to the Sun Gate, where sentries were once stationed to turn back those not permitted to set eye on the wonders laid out below. For me there are no sentries. Instead as I reach the Sun Gate for the first time a morpho butterfly, the size of a dinner plate and lit an electric lapis lazuli, the color of the sky condensed, flits up the path toward me and passes through the white stone pillars of the ruined archway. From here the path is all downhill, tired feet pattering down the paved pathway between banks of orchids that flourish as large as bushes and trees. Stepping down through such fragrance and color, I see that the ruined site still far below has grass that shines a bright light green, like the soft lawn of a garden. Surrounded by jagged Andean peaks, Machu Picchu resembles a place where mountains are tamed.

On my second visit to Machu Picchu, approached from below along a road that winds back and forth upon itself to gather height, our group arrives at dawn. We stand on a parapet and the tableau of land on which Machu Picchu is built seems like a yacht bobbing in a raging ocean. Clouds pour down from the highest peaks but they also stream up from the heights below. The mountains are darkness and the clouds are bright, as though ferrying daylight into the valley. Rimmed and packed with silver and white, they swirl and dance, rip to ribbons and re-form, drape the mountains and reveal them again—an astounding drama of immense scale. Our eyes shine and water as we stand and stare out, watching our planet breathe.

Don Pedro gathers us on a smooth rock carved into a landscape of its own, and we speak of the *apus*, the spirits of the mountains, for the first time. I wonder where *apus* stand in a cosmological hierarchy. Are they like angels, subservient to God?

I hear of Inti, the all-powerful god of the sun. I hear of Pachamama, a goddess we might view as Mother Earth. And I hear how *apus* feel no more regard for them than an industrialist might feel for an aristocrat. It takes a rare person, a sorcerer of exceptional training, to communicate with *apus*, because these mountain spirits have no interest at all in the ways of human beings. Some say that when the Incas abandoned the plateau of Machu Picchu this is the way they fled, their spirits leaping to join the *apus* on the highest peaks that even now are obscured by cloud. In fleeing, they took their secrets with them.

I wander the site, seeing what clues they left behind. A mountaintop is no place for humans to aspire to grandeur. The stonework of the buildings is impressive, the scale of the enterprise as it spreads over acres is daunting, but it is the intimacy of little details that strikes me. In the quarry are rocks that were being prepared for building even as the Incas left, cracks chiseled into great stones and filled with water to freeze in the night, ice expanding to split huge boulders into manageable blocks, water working stone. Climbing the trail a further fifteen hundred feet above the ruins, up to the summit of a peak also known as Machu Picchu, I notice that the ground is paved all the way and carved stone steps still give sure footing. This leaves me with tender thoughts of the human effort involved in hauling each one of the stones into place. And at the top, eleven thousand feet above the level of the seas, I see the summit has been worked into terraced gardens, where occasional flowers still grow.

A low hill rises from the site itself, an altar laid out on top, and from the surrounding walls juts a natural tip of rock. Looking from the contours of its pale stone to the contours of mountains that face it, you see that the one aspect mirrors the other.

Guidebooks proclaim how little is known about Machu Picchu, educated guesswork nibbling at the mystery and still coming away amazed, so I set my guidebook aside and see what the site can show me about itself. I ask that I be taken to what I should see. The process is simple, trusting my body to the same guiding force that led it during my time with ayahuasca some months before. Without the medicine my body is much heavier than then, I'm conscious of all the work involved in shifting my limbs, but in deciding to follow my feet my mind has no more decisions to take and so is free to trust and rest awhile.

My feet lead me down the slope from the altar, turn me to my right so that I leave the track and am walking over grass and then clambering up a waist-high step in the land, turn me round, and set me down. I look around and my mind kicks in again, making judgments.

"You're still as silly as they come," it says. "Look at you, plonked down in the middle of an undistinguished patch of grass. You ask to be led to something, and this is what it amounts to. When will you learn that abandoning control like that will lead you nowhere?"

With nothing more to say about a ridiculous situation, my mind turns silent and I sit on.

Simply sitting on the grass is pleasant enough. I look up at the blue of the sky, bring my gaze down to take in the mountains, down further still to take in the twin rocks that bulge from the grass in front of me. And then I understand. I am sitting in the very position from which it is possible to appreciate the wonder that these twin rocks hold. Looking from them to the twin peaks that rise behind them, I see that once again the rocks mirror the mountains exactly. They are angled the same way, their relative heights match the perspective from which I am viewing them, and even the deep fissure that marks the high peak to my right is marked in the same way on the right-hand stone.

I wonder if chance might have put them there. It seems unlikely, two such perfect stones in such perfect positions, the surrounding ground raised to be a viewing platform of the perfect height, but then Machu Picchu is a place for miraculous happenings. I turn around and look across to the hill that holds the altar on its top. At its ridge is the small run of stone in which I first noticed the reflection of the surrounding mountains. Now I am able to see it from the side, and recognize that the miniature mountain range jutting through the wall of the hilltop is simply the top few inches of a rock almost thirty feet deep and twenty feet wide. Made of a lighter stone, this giant rock has been set at an angle in the hillside, held in place simply so the patterns of one edge can protrude from the hilltop at the angle they do.

These reflections of the surrounding mountains are evidently neither accidental nor manufactured. It would be simple to carve a likeness of mountains from stone, and much simpler too to have broken off the corner of the mighty stone than to have raised and slotted the whole segment into the hillside. It seems clear that having recognized the forms of mountains within rocks, the ancient builders understood that those rocks were too sacred to break. The whole rock, whatever its size, needs to be set in place, and just as we see only the parts of a mountain that rise into the air so these rock replicas can be rooted far deeper in the earth than we would ever imagine.

. . .

"I like the perception," Carlos comments from his perch on the rock beside me. "I didn't see these reflective qualities in Machu Picchu especially, but then I find them everywhere. There are many mirrors in nature. But think of the effort, hauling vast rocks into place to mirror the surrounding mountains. Why do you think they bothered?"

"To show their admiration?"

"Always a good motive. But not enough in itself. You don't yet understand the nature of exchange. These Incan priests knew better. They wouldn't show their admiration without something in return."

"Isn't admiration already their part in the exchange? Their gift for what they admire?"

"True. But the cycle of exchange is endless. Reflect something, and you absorb its powers. That's why people sit in front of gurus. In reflecting the mountains, Machu Picchu is absorbing their energy into the earth. But tell me more. I'm revisiting the site as you speak. Enjoying your guided tour."

. . .

I stand up from the grass and tour the whole site, my eyes now trained to look for mountain forms in rocks, and again and again I find them. Looking from these rocks, I admire the exactness with which they reflect the contours and surface of the opposing mountain landscape.

At the center of this site, behind my back from where I was first led to sit, the ground drops to a lower level. There are no ruins on display here, though the hill with the altar complex stands to one side and the other is terraced and lined with a run of stone buildings. The ground below seems suited to an arena, spectators ranged on either side. A shallow pit rests in the middle of this area, but for me a greater clue to what might have happened here is the swath of grass of a different order from the grass elsewhere. I have noticed the same difference in old graveyards; thicker, paler grass growing where the minerals of decomposing human bodies alter the quality of the soil. It seems to me that the show witnessed by the spectators was a ritual of human sacrifice, human blood spilling its minerals into the surrounding ground.

Gathered alongside any human audience to watch this spectacle were the mountains. In recognizing that rocks were set to reflect the mountain landscape, I also see clearly that this site is now little more than a relic. No mystery remains to be discovered on Machu Picchu for the mystery has vanished. No coach-loads of tourists or archaeologists can reclaim it. The people who set the rocks dedicated their lives to the service and appreciation of mountains. The current of their lives is what flowed between these symbolic rocks and the distant peaks. Some lives were sacrificed to the knife, but all lives were sacrificed to the mountains, for there is nothing else to live for at such height. The rituals that enlivened Machu Picchu have been forgotten, but rituals are simply patterns learned from the daily commitment and focus of a person's life. It is the focus and appreciation of mankind that has gone, perhaps gone to play with the *apus* on the cloud-soaked summits.

Machu Picchu is a memorial to a time when we once held mountains in high regard. As a reward for that regard, the Incan civilization spanned this portion of the globe. Maybe the civilizations we have now are a reward for our disregard.

As the day closed, I joined the other travelers and we went back down the mountain.

. . .

Carlos unscrews the lid of the flask and pours me another cup of tea.

"So you think we've forgotten the mountains," he observes while I drink. "You think they've let us go."

The sun has risen during my story, and it strikes color from the summit of Canigou.

"I think so," I admit.

"So the Incas knew the secret of worshipping mountains, and now it's lost?"

"Maybe."

He passes me the monocular. I lift it to my eye, and Canigou leaps back into sharp detail.

"Awesome?" he asks.

I lower the monocular and nod.

"Excuse a dead man's wisdom, Martin, and let me tell you this. When something has roused you to awe, when it has felt the touch of your worship, it will never let you go. It's the case with mountains. It's the case with life."

We both stare out at the Pyrenean mountains in silence.

"So we're all right, then," I say. "The mountains are still looking after us."

"Far from it. They don't let go, but we can still fight to be free. Fight with our intelligence. See through the patterns that hold us. You know your Old Testament?"

"Only as stories. I've never studied it much. It doesn't appeal, to be honest. It's too full of war and vengeance, one tribe of Israel battling against another."

"So you understand? You see the pattern?"

I turn from the mountains to look at him, understanding nothing.

"Where do our myths start, Martin? The Garden of Eden, a place where four mighty rivers find their source, therefore obviously located up a mountain? Or after the Flood, where Noah leads man and beast down the slopes of Ararat? Does Judaism hail from the moment Moses receives the Ten Commandments on Mount Sinai? Or maybe it's when Abraham is spared the slaughter of his son Isaac on the summit of Mount Moriah, when the Lord of that mountain promises to secure the future of Judaism through Abraham's descendants.

"When the new Messiah arrives, of course he must make his appearance on Mount Zion and honor the prophecies that herald him. Jesus is born on the heights of Bethlehem. The devil leads him to a mountaintop for the last of his trials in the desert, and on such home ground Jesus has the power to resist. His disciples learn his worth after climbing with him to witness his transfiguration on the summit of Mount Tabor, his face flushed with light as Moses appears to him there and God speaks out of the clouds. He is crucified on a hilltop, on Calvary, and after his resurrection appears to his disciples on a mountainside in Galilee.

"Centuries pass and the Archangel Gabriel appears to a man sitting in a cave in the side of Mount Hira. The man is Muhammad, and it is in this mountainside that he first hears the words of the Koran. From the summit of Mount Moriah, where Abraham was pledged to obedience, Muhammad is later whisked on his night journey to the heavens.

Jews, Christians, Muslims, they struggle through the centuries, slay each other in thousands, for the right to lay claim to the heights of Jerusalem. In the name of God, Jews and Arabs, Christians and Moslems, Catholics and Protestants, regularly slaughter one another. Our planet stinks of religious massacres. Have you ever thought why?"

"It has to do with mountains?" I ask.

"One thing to know, before you give your heart to mountains. They are powerfully jealous of each other. Pledge loyalty to one and it expects you to be faithful. Followers of religions believe they are following the one God. They are wrong. History tells them they are wrong, the Bible tells them they are wrong, but they are slaves to their partial understanding and believe what they want to believe."

He raises his head toward Canigou, lifts his arms in salutation, and intones from the Bible in a clear-pitched voice.

"'I will lift up mine eyes to the mountain. From whence shall my help come? My help cometh from the Lord who made heaven and earth.'"

He lets the words resound awhile, then turns to me to continue his lesson.

"Devotees of religions worship the Lord of a mountain. They are the mountain's cohorts, and will battle the world to proclaim his dominion over the earth. Call it Islam, Judaism, Christianity, any faction, even the Mormons of America with their own message brought down from their own mountain, they are all mountain religions. Don't think mountains have let people go. Never think that. They have roused us with their prophets, stirred us with their myths, hidden themselves in our religions the way they hide themselves in cloud. They divide the peoples of the world among themselves, and set them at each other's throats."

I stay quiet for a while.

"Buddhism," I suggest after some thought. "That doesn't fit your theory."

"The one religion without a God. You're right. And where did it start? On a mountain? Uniquely, no, it didn't. The Buddha found his enlightenment under a tree. That doesn't mean mountains haven't done their best to take Buddhism over. Mountains of the Far East are clustered with Buddhist shrines. The slopes and peaks of Tibet are stacked with ridiculous Buddhist mythology. No matter what sect, choose your flavor of Buddhism, study real hard, and then see which jealous mountain god you've attached yourself to.

"But remember this feeling about Buddhism. Remember how it started under a tree when you move your story down from the Andes to the Amazon. Until the new American churches based around ayahuasca, no religion ever came out of the jungle. You can't separate the jungle religions from their trees, you see. And that's enough of my talking. Here endeth my sermon on the mount. Come, Martin. "

He stands and leads the way back down the path. I look east as we descend, away from the mountains, toward the strip of blue that is the Mediterranean Sea, and try and let its color wash me clean of so many alien thoughts.

6

THE BREAKFAST
MAGICIAN

At home in my kitchen he pulls the sleeves of his jacket back across the cuffs of his shirt, holds up his hands, and purses his fingers. He's making an exhibition of himself.

I watch, because in a house as tiny as mine any exhibition is hard to ignore.

His shirt is mustard yellow, made of thick brushed cotton and buttoned up to the collar. His jacket has the brown color of peat and something of the same texture. With a flourish he dips his hands into the two jacket pockets and plucks an egg out of each. These he places in a bowl on the sideboard. His hands dip into the pockets again, then again, till six large brown-shelled eggs are collected in the bowl. Then he reaches into his breast pocket and picks out a sprig of fresh parsley.

"Voilà!" he says. "Le petit déjeuner."

"Where did you get them?" I ask as he assembles the chopping board and knife and cracks the first of the eggs into a second bowl, whisking it as it falls.

"You have no ears?" He cracks all the eggs, deftly using just one hand while whisking with the other. "Didn't you hear the cockerel?"

"You took eggs from there? From the neighbor's hen-house? But that's stealing."

"The hens didn't complain. Why do you? Sit yourself down and finish your story while I cook."

"What story?"

"Machu Picchu. The story of coming down the mountain."

"I took the bus."

"And . . . ?"

. . .

The bus takes a road that zigs and zags down the mountain, working a gradual descent that drops twenty-five meters for every two hundred before turning a sharp corner back on itself to continue its descent.

A group of children gather at the first bend, shouting and waving at us. At the edge of the group stands a boy, a dark-skinned local of about fourteen dressed in a simple green tunic, a red headband round his shock of dark hair and a red belt round his waist, leather sandals on bare feet. He spreads his arms and leans to one side, like a bird banking in flight.

"Goodbye," he calls, his voice clear and the syllables long.

We smile and settle back in our seats as the bus continues, losing height, turning the first sharp bend.

"Goodbye."

Our boy is there again, poised in his stance of banked flight, emitting his long call, waiting for us to pass him on the road.

"Goodbye," again and again, a miraculous apparition every time our bus runs along a fresh straight. We rise from our seats to find him, wonder at how his trick is done, delight in the achievement. A race is on. Once we think we've beaten him, that our driver's raced the engine too fast and we'll be gone before he arrives, then he leaps through the undergrowth and lands on the road.

"Goodbye."

We passengers cheer. This is one race we don't want to win.

The bus turns a final bend, reaches the level of the river, and our descent is made. The boy jumps down to the road ahead of us and trots our way. The bus stops, the door opens, and the boy climbs in. Soaked in sweat, breathless, he holds on to the seats as he walks down the aisle, accepting money to fill a green bag tied to the belt around his waist.

"You paid him?" Carlos asks.

"More than I could afford."

"Nonsense. You paid for the two of us. That was a lovely story. It makes me happy."

He smiles as he continues his breakfast preparation. His obvious good mood is at odds with my bad one.

"Why did we have to speak of the mountains?" I ask. "Why so soon? Why before breakfast? And why frighten me with your version of religions? I don't need knowledge like that."

"What's better, a hen or a human?"

"That's a silly question."

"Then you'll give me a silly answer. Which of the two has a greater moral dimension?"

"Put that way it's easy. A human, of course. There's no morality in a hen."

"Wrong. Hens lay eggs. They do it whether I'm there to take them or not. They don't serve me. They serve their own nature. People have bigger brains than hens. Their scope is almost limitless. And what do they do with these great brains of theirs? They have ideas. And what's their next step? They serve those ideas. Hens conceive of no God, and slaughter nobody in God's name.

"Why do we two speak of mountains? We speak of mountains so we can learn from hens. We can follow their example, trust our own nature and be mindful of what it is that we serve.

"Your Peruvian boy of the mountains? He serves speed, youth, drama, surprise. This is vital, to serve the best of ourselves at any moment. In California your boy would be on the beach. There in the Andes he surfs the mountain. I like this boy. He brings to mind the young Carlos. It's time, I think, to reclaim that young Carlos. Time for tales of the jungle."

He puts a match to the gas ring on the stove. There is a whoosh as the blue flame sucks up the air and leaps four feet high.

"This is an old stove," Carlos observes.

"It's never done that before."

"Ha!" The flame has subsided to normal, but he waves his hands at it like a conjurer nevertheless. "There's life in the old dog yet, as they say."

He puts my old cast-iron pan on the heat and whisks the stream of beaten eggs as it flows into the pan. The eggs rise, he folds them, waits till the skin is mottled a light brown, slices the omelette in half, and presents it on two plates.

My first forkful stays solid as I lift it, then bursts in my mouth. The warmth, the taste, the juiciness are luscious.

"Magic," I say.

He smiles and cuts off a dainty mouthful for himself. We eat in silence as the sun wheels round to cast its light through the four-foot depth of the stone window casings and onto our table.

Carlos smacks his lips as the last morsel slides down his throat. "Impeccable, though I say so myself. Did you eat such delicacies in the jungle?"

"The food wasn't the highlight."

"You'll tell me. It will help us build a fresh appetite as we walk."

"I'll make up a picnic."

"How very European of you. We're going into the jungle. The jungle will feed us. We will take nothing but ourselves."

He stands, slides his chair under the table, and steps from the room. I hear him whistle a tune as he waits for me outside. His whistling is like a low wind, a seven-beat musical line that keeps repeating itself with variations. I clear the plates from the table and stack them in the sink, till the tune permeates me and I suddenly know where it comes from. It is the tune whistled by don Pedro, a tune of his own devising, sacred to the heart of the jungle ceremonies.

The light outside the front door is much brighter than any that filters through the jungle canopy. The air is much less humid. The summer has been dry, the river is narrow, the scrub and trees and bushes on the hills are turning brown, but as Carlos opens the gate and leads the way there is a very real sense of following him in through the first forest wall of the Amazon.

7

FOLLOW
THE LEADER

The gate was erected by the village commune, to stop small children from continuing on the path out of the village and tumbling to their deaths. Beyond it, and just outside my kitchen window, is a grating. The thin stream of an irrigation canal flows through it, traveling underneath the village to emerge again after a hundred yards, providing water for gardens and farming plots till it drops to rejoin the river.

When the grating clogs with leaves and twigs, the channel rises and tips over the wall as a waterfall. The course of the river runs some thirty feet below, beyond the rocks that form its banks. My job in the village when I am here is to keep this grating clean. I churn at it with a stick to stir the mat of leaves over the wall. Before I do, I feel through the water. Often I find a frog spread-eagled against the bars, the stream too fast to swim against, the drop over the wall too perilous to be an option of choice. I place the creature in a bucket and carry it down to where the river runs through bulrushes under the bridge. The frog keeps to the bucket's shelter as the river waters stream around it, till I pull the bucket away and it kicks its legs to move above the pebbles.

Carlos spins around on the narrow walkway beside the channel and dives toward my feet. With my back against the wall of the house, feeling the warmth already absorbed by its stone, I watch him scoop his hand through the water.

The creature on the palm of his hand is not a frog. It's a similar size, but far more curious. Four webbed feet, a stubby tail, skin a glossy black, but with flashes of vivid yellow zagged down its sides.

"What is it?" I ask.

A stupid part of me wonders if it's some creature he always carries with him, hidden up his sleeve, produced like this for moments of amazement. It isn't a creature that seems native to France, though I keep being surprised at the stark wildness of the Pyrenees.

Carlos lifts the creature to his ear. It waggles its feet in the air, then grows still as its head burrows into Carlos's earlobe.

"A fire salamander, it tells me." Carlos nestles the creature in his left hand and cups his right over the top. "Far from fiery now though. Chilled close to death by the water. It will accompany us a little way. Come on, Martin. This bodes well. There's adventure ahead of us."

I'm still wary of the narrowness of the path, and the sheer fall to the left of it. I worry at edging past the banks of wild fennel that grow in a wild garden to my right. Carlos steps out with a nimbleness I glance up to admire before looking back down at my feet. He waits for me beneath the shade of an ancient cherry tree, whose trunk is rooted ten feet below so that its branches drape a low canopy over the path.

He takes a deep breath as I catch up with him, then lets it out. It is a sigh of contentment.

"A perfect day in a perfect world," he says.

. . .

I let out a sigh too, but of a different kind. I don't notice I've done so till he turns to me with a question.

"Sorry for yourself or for the world?"

"Neither. Just unsettled."

"By me?"

"I suppose so. I was happy till you came. This village generally makes me happy. I felt out of balance till I got back here. A few walks in the hills set me to rights again. Now that balance is gone. Even this walkway seems narrow and dangerous. What have you done, Carlos? I walk this way every day. Now I feel that if I take one more step I will fall."

He stares at me a moment. I worry about what he is preparing to say, but his lips barely move when he speaks and his voice is soft.

"Sit down."

Steps lead down around the cherry tree to a garden plot below. I tread down the first one and sit down beside the channeled stream.

"Your heart is beating fast?" Carlos asks.

"Knocking. Really hard. It feels just this side of a heart attack."

"It's exhilaration."

"It's fear."

"Same thing."

"Not in my world, Carlos. Not in my world."

"Then leave your world. You have to. You know this. You have to step through your fear."

"Fear can be good. It stops you jumping in front of a train. Stops you walking off a cliff."

"This little walkway is the path that you tread every day, you tell me. Is it a rational fear that sees you terrified of this path?"

It's obviously not rational. Fear doesn't have to be rational to be real, I am about to reply. Instead I sit and think a while longer, till I come up with a rational response.

"I'm scared of following you."

"Ha!"

Carlos manages to sit himself down on the narrow strip of cement beside the channeled water. He uncovers the salamander and settles it on the palm of his right hand, his middle finger crooked as a support for the reptile's chin. His left hand he places against my chest.

"Your heart's beating fast enough for two." He takes his hand away. "That's what hearts do at the point of entering a new relationship. It happened to me on meeting my teacher."

"Is it happening now?"

"I feel the pressure on your heart as my own. Otherwise not. You should have felt my heart that day in Cuzco though, when you spoke my name and then breathed me in. I certainly did. Boom. Boom. I thought I would die. For a moment I did."

"You died?"

"Just for a moment."

"Is this something you've been doing all your life? Dying and resurrecting yourself?"

"You're being flippant, Martin." He lets the silence carry a gentle rebuke for a while, before continuing. "But yes. We die many times in one lifetime. People are stuck on death as something final, whereas it's just a transition. Our lives are put on hold many times. Our spirit pops out to check the terrain and often discovers radical new departures. Our bodies are heavy and our habits are strong, so of course we normally ignore such chances to change and carry on in our old ways. But those little deaths keep on coming, till the big one arrives that can't be ignored. I say that, though of course people do ignore it as long as they can. So many people I've met out there do not realize they have died."

"You say things like that and expect me to follow you? It's like taking a hike with death."

"We all take hikes with death. It makes our lives exquisite. But you are afraid, so here is what we shall do. We shall sit and stare at the path ahead. When it looks ready for us, we shall stand up and walk. I tell you now, the path will be ready for me and I shall walk along it. If it looks ready for you, you walk along it too. If it doesn't, turn around and go back home. You will never see me again. If we both walk the path, whoever goes first, the other must not go in the spirit of following. No one is a follower, no one a leader. We are simply both alive."

I look at him to see if he is going to say more, but he simply stares at the path. The salamander on his hand shares the same focus.

I look ahead and stare too.

• • •

I don't know how many minutes elapse before the first effect kicks in. Maybe fifteen. Then there is no sense of time. No sense of Carlos or the salamander either. Simply a view of the changing path.

I suspect what I see is dazzles of light, bounced as reflections from the flowing stream. They are bright shimmers, glints that stretch out through the air and then fade. I know heat haze, when the view above the ground wobbles out of shape. This change in the air has no such loss of definition, no waves of shapelessness. It is more as if the air were defining itself as crystal.

The glints spread wider, building on themselves like the structure of cells. I look to the thin channel of water running as the center of the path to pass by my side, understanding now that the light is no reflection, and I see that the quality of the stream has changed. The sound of its running is clear to me, in fact it is amplified to the volume of a torrent as I listen, but for a while the water looks quite still. Then I notice movement begin, and it is a dual movement. The stream has twin currents. One is the usual flow, the surface heavings and churnings of the water coming toward me. The other is a pointillist version of the same water, like a vision of its atomic structure, and this is flowing too, only it flows upstream.

And as a stream can flow against itself, so the cement pathway on either side of the channel is on the move too. Solid turns to liquid, and the atomic structure flows up against its own gradient.

I look up from the path to the crystallized air, and find it has taken the form of solid light. It arches above and around the path, like a tunnel in that it stretches into the distance, but unlike a tunnel in that it gives no sense of boundaries. There is no light at the end of this tunnel, for the tunnel is light.

I stand, step forward, and place a foot on either side of the water. The path is solid, the movement still flowing but forming no conveyor belt. The path has direction but movement along it has to be my own.

I see Carlos is right. Fear can be exhilaration.

Step by step, I walk the path and journey into the light.

. . .

I sense Carlos sitting down beside me.

"You put something into those eggs?" I ask. Opening my eyes, I turn to him and smile.

He smiles back. I lean forward to look beyond him, along the short section of path we have both walked. The ancient vine terraces, earth piled high behind walls of rounded stone, rise to the left. To the right are the wild pomegranate and fig trees. The channel carries water in between them. The cement to either side of the channel is solid, weathered, static. The view has assumed its old, accustomed form.

Below our feet a mountain stream tumbles down to the river. We are sitting on a bridge, a basic one built of flagstones that carries the path and channel over the dip in the land. We are in the shade of a younger cherry tree that grows on the level above us. I swing my legs, look down into the dark green shadows of the foliage, and can find nothing to say.

"Let me tell you a story," Carlos says, and sets the docile salamander down on his trouser leg so that his hands are free to draw illustrations in the air. "It's an ayahuasca story. It asks to be told now."

. . .

"I am sitting, like this, but on a rock beside a river. Think of it as this river below us, only twice as wide and faster flowing. Maybe I've been sitting for an hour. Maybe for a lifetime."

"Is this in France? Here in the Pyrenees?"

68

He pauses at my interruption, and stares into my face as though willing me to apologize.

"No. Peru. If you have any more interruptions in you, use them now."

"Is this story a dream, or something real?"

"Your question saddens me. I will repeat it to you at the end of my tale. Hopefully you will have found your own answer. Till then, though I may speak, I shall not speak to you. I shall address my tale to the fire salamander. She is already rapt and most receptive. Eavesdrop if you wish."

Carlos turns his attention from me, and tells the rest of his tale in words that sail out over the salamander's head.

"I am on a rock. It was hot to sit on, but now the heat has passed into me and there is comfort so long as I keep still."

His head erect, his eyelids closed, he journeys into the memory. I hear a noise, a slow and grinding roar, and look around. The noise continues, and I trace it to his throat. As I do so, his eyes snap open and he stares directly ahead.

"The noise is unlike any I have ever known. Only the vision before me explains it. A rock stands at the edge of the river, water streaming around it. As I watch a small bump on the top of the rock it swells, it grows, and I see that the sound I am hearing is the sound of growing stone.

"The bulge rises to take the shape of a helmet, the sort of smooth leather helmet worn by early aviators. This helmet is molded to the skin of the creature that appears beneath it. As the head is lifted higher on top of shoulders and a torso, I watch the creature's eyes. They are the large round eyes of an owl, but set in the eye sockets of a man's face. I say a man, but he is more like the original of garden gnomes, his flesh and clothing all an unpainted gray stone.

"I expected him to keep on rising, but his legs when they appear swell out of the sides of the rock. He is straddling it, the river water mounting round his feet.

"My rock is on higher ground, so he has to look up at me. His eyes engage mine. The pupils are gray but flecked with black, and as I look at these black specks they shift and take wing into a flight of crows. The crows in flight are my whole field of view for a moment. When the view clears the creature has his back to me, and somehow the land between us has risen so that our two rocks are joined into one vessel. He kicks with his feet and our ship of rock starts to move.

"I grip at stone with my hands, shift my legs to cling to the sides, and instinctively kick out with my feet to help propel us forward. Our vessel enters the river and races on top of its flow."

Carlos's body judders with the impact of his tale. His presence as a narrator is too distracting for me. I cannot watch him while picturing the images of his story for myself. I close my eyes as he continues:

Life's a strain sometimes. Then it all turns around. The best you can do is hold on for the thrill of the ride.

I'm holding now. Speed is a blur of white and blue and green around me, and a rush of cool wind against my face. The force of the wind increases to buffet my whole body as the creature in front of me melts. Inch by inch he retreats back into the stone. I draw my feet out of the water to rest them where his body has disappeared, lean back on my hands, and look ahead.

The way ahead is a wave of white water spurting over our bow. The vessel gathers speed, we are on a steeper incline, and for a moment of panic I see that the fate of the creature is to be my own fate. The way ahead is now nothing but stone, a mountain of granite wider than the horizon and reaching up to mask the sky.

My hands slip. Flat on my back, I wait for the moment of impact.

It comes, but without pain. It is an enveloping darkness.

I think to rise, to explore this sudden afterlife. In front of me is nothing but blackness. I look behind, and sight returns. The river rushes my way, dipping through the narrow opening of a cave to turn subterranean. I watch the water flow till it reaches my vessel, and see that my rock is now a ledge and the water rushes beneath me.

There is no chance of stepping in and wading back to the light. The power of the water is much too full. I turn again to the way ahead, and the darkness has lifted.

Or rather, as in the cinema, an image has projected itself upon it.

My rock merges with the land as a beginning of an illumined path.

Gloom hangs to my left, but as I walk it configures itself as shadows, and these shadows group together into the trunks and branches of a forest. A song winds its way through the trees, its clear notes formed from a woman's voice to keep pace with my progress. I catch sight of her white robe, the flowing tresses of her hair that blend the reds, the blues, the orange hues of a fire's flames, and though I cannot see the details of her face her grace compels me to love her.

I love her for her height too. As I look up to the stars, look up to the mountains, I like to look up to my women.

A woman more than six feet tall is liable to excite me. This apparition seems to vary in height, but is eight feet at her shortest. She is my type of woman.

Her unattainability makes her still more so. Her identity is clear to me. Clear in the way a baby knows its mother at its first glance out into the world. She is the lord and mistress of the forest, the mother of ayahuasca, and her song unwinds like the supplest of vines.

A song and a vision such as this should enchant me, but I am wary of enchantment. I turn my head to the right of the path, and peer out into the dusk. At first there is nothing but grayness to see. Then I peer down, and find that the land lies an unscalable distance below me.

It is a barren stretch, with little vegetation and many rocks. From my elevation I see nothing to wonder at, but below me there are groups of people engrossed in their lives. With arms looped around each other and their bodies stooped to bring their heads close, they seem to be keeping a secret, and they turn now and again to check on other groups. All around the barren land such clusters stoop and peer about.

The people are draped in clothes of drabness, a camouflage against the terrain. There is nothing to appeal in what I see but for the configurations of a game. Yet their excitement in the game, though restrained, is very clear. It is the excitement to be found when greed anticipates fulfillment, a static excitement that almost chokes upon itself. The path descends and I descend with it, approaching for a closer look.

They see me now, and their game comes to a halt. Faces turn my way, and arms are drawn back. They pre-

*pare to throw me something. I prepare to catch it. As I
do so a song from the forest draws my attention.*

I turn back to the other side of my path.

*The mother of ayahuasca is close now. Her face is
simply a green wash of forest colors but her robe is bril-
liant in its whiteness and her flaming hair is vivid. Its
tips are licks of blue and the air around her is white with
heat. I hear the tune of her song, then find it has unrav-
eled to leave words I can understand.*

"Where . . . ," she sings,

"are . . .

"you . . . ?"

*The players below me shout for my attention. They
use a name that they seem to think is mine. The name is
their gift to me, and their hands hold out other offer-
ings. The gifts are sticks, a rarity in their rocky land
where wood does not appear to grow..*

*"Who are these people?" I ask the forest lady. My
words come from me in song, and conjure a song in
return.*

> *"People like you*
> *Who took the path.*
> *Reached where they are*
> *But no further.*
> *They followed desires*
> *But not their feet.*
> *Look*
> *where you are going."*

*Though my voice now sings, it doesn't have the meter of
verse. "How did they get down from the path?" I ask.*

"*They play a game*
That's less than life.
They play a game.
They play a game."

A stick lands at my feet, and stirs up dust like tinsel
spray. I bend toward it.
A line of song arrests my motion, and I pause to wait
for the sense of its message.

Shamans in a shadow land
See them cock their heads,
Ears attuned to silent whistles
From their magic darts.
Look. You have one at your feet.
An invitation to the game.
Pick it up
To enjoy
Eternities of playing.

"*Is it fun?*" *I ask.* "*Is it fun to play their game?*"

This dusk you see
Masks nothing.
What you see is what there is
In all its radiance.

"*And this stick?*" *I ask.* "*What should I do with it?*"

Pick it up
And they succeed.
Before you engage

Consider.
Do you choose to play this game
Or do they choose you?

I consider the stick. It doesn't seem threatening. A stick might well be useful along a forest path.

"If I walk past this stick, and do not pick it up," I ask her, "how far along the path might I go?"

Her song, wordless now, streams off into the depths of her forest. I look down at the players of the game. They are animated now. Their faces break into silent laughter, they jump in the air and twirl around, making their game attractive. The air seems to shift and spin around them, like a torrent of tiny insects.

A boulder is lodged on the forest side of my path. I sit on it for reflection.

As my decision forms itself, I feel the warmth of the sun against my face and the heat of stone beside my legs. I open my eyes. My view is of the river from where I sit on the rock. The sunlight is gentle as it dips below the landscape, placing colors on the river as the water rushes by.

Carlos slides a finger down the fire salamander's spine.

"So there's my story," he tells her. "Do you think our friend was listening too?"

He turns to me. His eyes are moist with unshed tears.

"So, Martin, dream or reality?"

"That was no dream." I get used to the view across the river, the play of sunlight across the field of low vines, the children's playground with its bright yellow slide in front of the modern village hall. It feels right to anchor myself in a view of a world I am used to before continuing. "It was a story without an end, though. Did you pick up the stick?"

"It's important to hear the question. Not my answer. You have to make the choice for yourself."

"But did you?"

"You have too much sense of Carlos Castaneda, for all that you have not read my books. Too many expectations. Please let them go. I am beyond that now. But I'll answer you. No, I did not pick up the stick."

"But you entered the game?"

"Ha!" He wipes his eyes with the back of his hands, and is grinning when he turns to me. "See! Already you know my actions as well as your own! Yes, you're right. I am a proud rather than a stupid man. I thought I could have the best of both worlds. I did not stoop and pick it up, but still I joined the game. The mother of ayahuasca was right. That game-world was a hard place to leave. I tell you this, Martin. Shamanism is not a spectator sport. Come, let's continue our walk. I'm all talked out. Our legs need to get some more conversation pumping."

"Along the path?"

"Why not? I'm free of distractions. Let's see how far we can go."

He cups the salamander in his hands, and steps out.

8

THE HARMONY
OF BRAINS

The path skirts a hillside, wheeling round to the left. Its curve follows even as it exaggerates the bend in the river. The rivulet carried wide to ferry water to the village still runs beside our feet. To our left is the rough lawn surrounding the first of two mill houses. Until recently two dogs, one with the looks and injured ferocity of a jackal, would bark and snarl greetings at this juncture of the walk while the washing of a single woman's vast brood, the eldest a soldier back from the Balkans and the youngest tiny golden-tressed twins, spanned the garden on a long clothesline. Now the dogs, the colors of the wash, the blond mother resplendent in her one-piece scarlet swimsuit, are gone. The family was evicted for nonpayment of rent, and the house is emptied, ready for sale.

I tell Carlos this as we walk. Then I speak of the latest developments in the boundary dispute between the village and the second mill house that we pass. The English owners, friends of mine, are sitting in the shade of an apple tree in their garden and fail to see me when I wave.

About thirty people weather each winter in the village. I used to think of them as hardy old souls, too impoverished to afford retreats in the gentler climate of the Mediterranean coast, battening their ancient doors and stoking the fires in their kitchen-cum-front-rooms, holding out for the spring. On closer acquaintance I learned of the domestic and sexual intrigues that render even these old and sequestered mountain lives both warm and spiced. And in the summer the population swells to more than two hundred; shutters slam open and breezes breathe through the houses as families return from the far removes of Parisian lives to make a holiday playground of their ancestral village.

This day in August is at the height of the holiday period. One spring I was excited by the village dogs' quest for bitches in heat. I watched their comings and goings along the dusty lanes, sad there was no one to share my dog gossip with, then recognized how pinched my world had become. Now, for this brief period, the matrix of passions and intertwined desires that gives energy to city life is transplanted to our village. The whole valley is in heat, and we watch each other with excitement.

Carlos breaks the flow of my village gossip by stepping from the pathway and down a wooded slope. I follow, holding on to the trunks of slender trees for balance, and stop beside Carlos. He is looking through the trees at the people gathered below. Sand has been trucked up into the mountains, then tipped and raked to form a beach. Thirty feet wide and twenty feet deep, the beach is already fairly covered with families and beach towels. Bodies ranging from white through pink to bronze sit and lie in the blaze of the sun. An overspill of people is in the water.

If they all looked up they would see us. They don't.

"They're playing games," I remark to Carlos, reminded of his story. "They've fallen off the path."

"You're an idiot," he informs me. "That story I told our salamander here is a vision of the shamanic path. It is quite specific. I don't deal in metaphors."

The outdoor rock pool, almost circular and a quarter of an acre in size, is a natural delight of the village. The river tumbles in from the southwest. Boulders coated mineral white give the look of a sizable waterfall even when the river is low. The pool is deep enough in parts to accept high dives. A small ledge forms a diving platform in the rock face to one side, and steps are hammered up the side of a tree that leans out above the water from the side where we stand.

Two adults, a male and a female, slice a crawl back and forth across the widest section of the pool. Two women lounge in the shadows. And three children are stationed around the rocks.

"Do you know the triune brain theory?" Carlos asks.

"You tell me I'm an idiot. How could I know such a thing?"

He ignores my sulks and shifts straight into his explanation.

"Man has three brains. The most ancient and smallest, lodged in the bump you feel at the top of your spine, has been with us since our reptilian existence. It's our lizard brain. The second, domesticated and obedient, that coats the first like short-cut pastry, is our dog brain. The third, some say the highest but also the youngest and largest and most tender of all, is the thick mass that we know as gray matter. Dogs have the lizard brain as part of their makeup as well, but of all the mammals this gray matter is unique to us. That's why it's called the human brain. And below us are three children to illustrate the theory. Do you see that girl?"

She is maybe fourteen. Of the three children, she is doing the least to attract attention to herself. Yet her tactics as an attention-grabber are superb.

She is lying on the flattened top of a rock about seven feet above the pool, her arms at her sides, her legs straight out. Before lying down she must have arched her back and reached her hands around her long black hair to lift it high, for it is set around her head as it would float were she on her back in the water.

Thin cotton straps hold triangular black cups that pouch her breasts, which have the fresh plumpness of something still growing. A patch of black material forms her briefs, tied against the flesh of her sides with bows. The costume is as close to nudity as she dares. The sun ripens her as she lies quite still, absorbing the heat to her core.

"She's illustrating the lizard brain," Carlos says.

"You think that's what she's doing?" I ask. "Are you fully returned from the dead?"

A pulse goes through the girl. Her head lifts up, her left foot slides along the rock to raise her inner thigh into view, and she lowers the sunglasses from her eyes to stare over them.

She is looking at a newcomer, who stands in the shade of the trees beyond the beach. And he looks back. Aged sixteen, trainers on bare feet, baggy shorts hanging down to his kneecaps, a lilac muscle shirt loose around his body, his hair the brown fuzz of his summer cut, the youth returns her look.

"The lizard brain, home to the basic instincts," Carlos opines. "Lust, hunger, fear, aggression. The flash points in our behavior, those times when we snap and lose our control, they all surge out of the lizard brain. It strips us of pretensions and leaves us bare-bones naked. Now, you see *that* boy?"

He could easily be the brother of the girl on the rock, judging by her total disregard for him. Her younger brother, about twelve years old. Where she is stillness, he is movement. His body, a glossy bronze but for the electric blue of his swimming trunks, spread-eagles against the rock face as he finds the hand- and footholds to haul himself up from the water to the diving ledge. Once there, he turns his head. On the beach his mother, sitting upright in her one-piece swimsuit of fluorescent pink, gives him her full attention.

The boy reaches back his arms. His posture promises a beautiful swallow dive. As his knees flex he looks across to his mother. Makes sure she is watching. The promise of flight becomes a loss of balance. His legs pedal through the air and his body smacks against the water.

His mother looks shocked by the splash, then reverts to a smile when her son's head appears. He finds his bearings by seeking her out again.

"The dog brain's active in that one," Carlos continues. "Trust, loyalty, obedience, friendship, play. Even much of what we know as love. Now observe this girl beneath the trees."

She sits on a rock in the shade below us. Thirteen most likely, her blond hair tucked behind her ears. Though she is in the shade, she still wears loose drawstring pants down to her ankles and a full-sleeved cotton blouse as protection against the sun. Her legs are crossed, and cradled in her lap is a book. Comfortable in the landscape, she is somewhere far away in spirit. Carlos picks up a short stick and lobs it into the water in front of her, as though it were falling naturally from the tree. Its splash makes her jump. She traces the disturbance to the stick, watches the rings from the splash eddy toward her on the shore, then returns to her book and its faraway setting.

"This girl is steered by the human brain. The stirring of art, of music, of science, of philosophy, the capacity for a moral viewpoint, the perspective of setting oneself apart, all stem from this gray matter. You're with me so far?"

"Is this a metaphor, or are there actually three brains?"

"As I said, I don't deal in metaphors. For want of a better word, this is science. Paleocortex, mesocortex, and neocortex. A big trouble with people, maybe the basic one, is that we are run from one brain at a time rather than all three in harmony. Promptings from the lizard brain result in our rashest actions, not a damn given for the consequences. That's our kill-or-be-killed, devil-take-the-hindmost mode. The dog brain sees us mawkish and flabby-minded, eager to go with the herd. And the human brain on its own is doomed to self-reflection. 'How does this experience reflect on me?' is its constant reaction. Life from the outside in rather than the inside out. Come now, Martin. You're in storytelling mode. Tell me a story of someone acting one brain at a time."

There's power in a request for a story. You're no longer rattling anecdotes into a vacuum. Your story is invited to engage with someone's life. It will mix with the listener's experience, and the chemistry of that mixture can have the power to heal. It's important to pause, let go of expectations, and see what story might emerge.

My head clears itself at Carlos's request, and only one story comes to mind. I wait, so much wanting an alternative story to reveal itself, but nothing comes. It is this story or nothing. And as I tell the story, I recognize that I am also its listener.

. . .

"This story belongs to Glasgow in the week of the first air strikes in the Gulf War. It happened on a day when all the world was turned upside down. A day when hell smothered the life of my friend.

"He was an artist who worked as my illustrator. I knew him as bright, sensitive, caring, a good husband to his young wife and good father to his baby daughter. The other love in his life was a 1973 Porsche Targa. It was red, so he called it Scarlet, and spoke lovingly of the car's feminine curves.

"He nursed it from a wreck back to pristine condition. Weekdays it stayed under a tarpaulin on the street outside his house. Saturdays he could always find an extra hour or two to care for it. The engine gleamed as bright as the body. On Sunday mornings the wraps came off again and he drove his family off to visit with either his parents or his in-laws.

"That day they were nearly there, just turning into the main street that leads to his parents' house, and a battered Ford shot out in front of them. Two thirteen-year-old joy-riders were in the front seats. They were using the white center markings like a track. There was no room for my friend to stay on course. He swerved onto the sidewalk, tried to straighten but couldn't, and the Porsche scraped its side along a wall.

"That should have been it. Some shock for the family, a reparable car. But that's not how it was. When his wife talks now, she talks only of this. How the man she had lived with and loved became someone she had never seen. His face contorted, yelling curses, slamming his foot down on the pedal and bombing his Scarlet to top speed. His wife screamed, his baby cried, and he just kept shouting as the engine mounted into its air-cooled roar and they drew close to the tail of the road-hogging Ford.

"It lasted minutes—maybe two, maybe three. Maybe the kids didn't know their road signs, maybe they panicked, but they veered up a road and my friend followed. It was the exit ramp to the highway. Both cars flew at top speed into the lanes of oncoming traffic.

"The stainless steel roll bar on the car saved the wife's life, but her story becomes a blank at this point. All she knows is that she woke up in a hospital as a childless widow. The teenage joyriders died too, as did one other driver caught in the pileup."

. . .

"Will that do?" I ask Carlos.

He simply returns my look.

"The dog brain for the love of his wife, his daughter, maybe even his car? The lizard brain for the curses, the madness, the life-busting surge of road rage? The human for his artistic side, his pride in that perfect, damnable Porsche? I still can't connect that driving demon to the careful friend I'd known. Perhaps there wasn't one person. Perhaps there were three, governed by three brains as you say, and I simply never met them all. What happens in death, Carlos? Do all these fractured parts come together?"

"Please finish your story."

So I go quiet for a while, discovering what is left to tell.

"It's not just that we act from only one brain at a time," I realize. "We can take in only one aspect at a time as well."

For I remember and recount how others dealt with the death.

. . .

They buried the baby, and after an autopsy they buried my friend. His wife stayed away. There were maybe fifteen of us gathered in the plain funeral parlor of the Scottish crematorium. The coffin was shrouded in a purple velvet cloth. After an address was given and prayers spoken, machines cranked and the coffin was lowered, the cloth falling flat as the bulge of the coffin sank from sight. And with the dropping of the coffin and the body into the furnace below I sensed a rushing upwards, a huge release as the soul of my friend flew from the scene.

Outside, I joined the line of people waiting to pay their respects to my friend's parents. The man and woman, my friend's features shared between them, were not old themselves. They stood in black outfits, smiled their thanks for our coming, and shook our hands. In childhood their son had suffered from a heart complaint. Maybe this was linked to the road rage. I don't know. As he roamed the Scottish hills they feared he might never return. But surgery and medical care saw him through to a sweet life. And now this.

"How can they survive?" I asked the minister.

"They absorb what they can, and leave the rest," he reassured me, recalling all the other people he had counseled through grief. "This is nothing they can comprehend, so they don't even try. We'll never know how they can survive, but believe me, they will."

To try and reach my own understanding, I visited the city library and ordered all the newspapers of the previous week. The story was a second-lead to the Gulf War stories but was easy to find. As I read all the versions in the press there was not a scrap of my friend to be seen in all the reportage. Simply a story of a road-rage maniac locked on revenge who brought death to several families on a Sunday morning. One more pulse of horror in a city accustomed to violence.

. . .

"Thank you," Carlos says. "I don't know what to do with your story. Can we just walk on a little way, and see what comes to me? It's time to release this little creature in any case."

The salamander seems settled for now on the open palm of Carlos's right hand. He carries her back to the cement pathway and follows it to its end. This is where the stream of water is diverted from the river, angled to run along the irrigation channel. There is nowhere else for us to walk, but at shoulder height is a ledge broad and long enough to be a path for our reptile. Carlos sets her down and she immediately scuttles along and out of sight.

"Au revoir," he says.

He leans back against the side of the hill, and looks up through overhanging branches toward the blue of the sky.

"You ask me if all the parts of ourselves come together in death. We will find that out in time. Crucial for now is that you pull together the fractured parts of yourself before we carry on.

"We're about to walk into history. You'll find yourself intact when we get there, but it's better if you can take with you a little extra prescience to illuminate the figure you were then, otherwise the venture will be a waste of time. We'll not change history. Simply take a little more consciousness to it, knowing where it's heading.

"The trick of bringing the three brains into harmony is to open up to infinity. Invite down a force that sees you acting according to its designs. It's the equivalent of opening up to our potential on this earth. That's what our free will amounts to: opening ourselves fully to the plan that's laid out for us. You know some of this, so I won't belabor it.

"What pleases me most about the story of your friend, and it does please me even as it tires me out, is your reaction to the newspaper stories. You saw the depth behind the sensationalism. You learned that there is infinitely more to a story than its details, even though sensational details are all that most readers want. Those newspapers offered facts but couldn't get near the truth.

"I pulled this story from you, in place of the trite stuff you were feeding me, because I knew you needed to hear it. Admit it, you'd forgotten about your friend."

He lowers his head to look at me, and I nod.

"It threw me for a while," he continued. "I knew the story, as I know everything in your life, but I also knew you had forgotten it. Then I remembered your naiveté. You've never learned the essence of a storytelling life. Shall I tell you it?"

I nod again.

"Collect and recount the stories that shaped you. Until you do, you'll never be properly shaped. Life is a storytelling art form. Censorship is evil but editing's divine. There are not so many episodes that define a life. If you fail to recollect them, let alone learn from them, your life will never be defined. This story of your Glaswegian friend is a fundamental one for you. You thought his life blessed, and discovered it cursed. It showed you there was no model for your life but your own. And left to your own devices, with nothing to model yourself on that you could trust, you were completely at a loss. You sold your apartment and belongings and set off on the search, the quest, that has led you to this moment. Led you to talking to me by this riverside here and now. Am I right in this, or am I fantasizing?"

"You're right."

He lets out a deep sigh.

"Forgive me," he explains. "I hate preaching. But time is limited and there's only so much narrative I can push myself through. Now remember as we step into history that your life has no models. There is nothing to trust. On your own, life can be spurred by only one brain at a time. To have the three brains run in harmony you have to give up control. Know that, and in history we'll see where you failed."

"We're looking for my failures?"

"Don't worry. Failure's a byproduct of success, and who really cares about either? We're looking for something much more juicy. Come with me."

. . .

Carlos takes off his shoes, ties the laces together and hangs a shoe either side of his shoulder, and steps his stockinged feet into the river.

"What are you doing?" I ask.

"There's no going back on this route. Ever onward, Martin. Ever onward. I shall stand here till you join me, or till I get swept away. The choice is yours."

The river is some twenty-five feet wide at this point, and just a few feet from where Carlos is standing it drops into a weir. I have sometimes come and sat mesmerized by the smooth curve of water as the river eases over its fall. I've never thought to use this as a crossing place though.

I tie my trainers and hang them over my shoulder to copy Carlos, and step into the water. The force of the current snatches at my ankles. I make my way, stone by stone, to stand at his far side. I'm heading for the far bank and haven't thought to stop, but he yells in my ear.

"Turn and face upstream!"

As he yells he takes hold of my shoulder and spins me round. His shout starts a roar in my ear, the sound of the river falling over the weir but amplified to a level of pain. His hand supports my back as I lose my balance. I seem to be falling even as the view in front of me stays in place. I see the waters of the river, and the high reach of trees to its sides.

Then the roar subsides to little more than a babble, and the cold flow around my ankles grows warm. I notice high mud banks to either side, and see how the riverbed of stones has disappeared beneath the brown stream of the water. The river, a warm river, is churning mud into its course.

And then the pieces slot together. I am losing my mind even as the scene in front of me begins to make sense. I stepped into a river in the French Pyrenees, but I am standing in a river in the Amazon.

The pressure of Carlos's hand on my back increases, and I let myself fall against it.

9

UPRIVER

A rock brings me back. In my hand it is a lightweight shell twice the size of my fist, curved like my fist too and with a pinkness to match the flesh of my palm. It is clearly the shell of a snail, though the Amazonian creature that once lived here redefines the species with its size. It would be a feast in itself for any Frenchman.

I press my hand hard around it, hard enough to crush it to splinters. Instead of breaking, the shell presses into my flesh. It is solid, and the warmth leaks from it until it is cold and has transmitted that cold to my entire body.

My eyes open against a blue sky. The pain in my hand makes me release my grip on what is no longer a shell but a rock. Water surges broad and strong around me, tugging and pulling at my body, twisting it round. My head is the only anchor, the only thing keeping me in place. I jerk it forward, turn from my back to reach for the ground with my hands and knees, find my face is submerged and water is filling my nostrils.

"Up!"

The shout gives me a clue how to orientate myself. Carlos's hands provide another. They were holding my head, but now they grab me under the armpits and haul me from the river. My feet drag against the stones till he has dropped me on the riverbank.

The riverbank in the French Pyrenees.

I blink and rub the water from my eyes and look out across the weir, to the path we had followed on the other side.

"Come on," Carlos says. He is wet too, his trousers soaked though his top half is relatively dry. "Come up and rest till your senses come back."

I haul myself out of the water and sit down next to him. Neither of us speaks for some time.

"Sorry," he finally says. "I'm so fixed on knowing every aspect of your life I lose sight of the fact that you and I are not the same person. There is so much your body does not know yet. Simple things. Such as balance."

"I can balance," I say. "It's not my forte, I admit. I used to fall over and walk into things a lot, but I'm much better than I was. I watch where I'm going, try not to walk backwards, that sort of thing. I can regress when I'm tired, become flat-out Mr. Magoo then, but I'm nowhere near as clumsy as I was. Put me in any real-life situation and I can cope. Flash me bodily to another continent while I'm standing in the middle of a European river and then maybe things do fall apart. What's your game, Carlos? How do you do that?"

"Do what? Tell me what happened."

"You know what happened. You tempted me into this river, then pulled some trick that flashed me back six months so that I thought I was standing in an Amazonian stream. How did you do that?"

"Recall your own actions before you go questioning me. You think that was a flashback to a different time?"

"I was walking upriver to the jungle clearing. It shocked me at first, then I remembered it clearly."

"Were you on your own or with others?"

"On my own."

"And that's what you did six months ago? Went walking in the river on your own?"

I was never on my own in that stretch of river, but always in a party of others. I see the nature of the question, see that he needs me to think rather than reply.

"So that wasn't a memory?" I eventually ask.

"Real time, Martin. The Peruvian Amazon in the here and now. And much as you've sworn in recent weeks that you'll never go back, I worried for a while that I'd never be able to drag you out of there. Whatever you did in the jungle, Martin, it grabbed hold of you. It's part of you now."

"Did you see it? Did you see what I was seeing?"

"For a while. I walked with you for a while. I was part of your enchantment as you looked up toward the jungle canopy, rubbed the moisture from leaves against your cheeks, squeezed the mud between your toes. Then you entered the waterfall, the thin stream that showered down from rocks to your left, cool water cascading across the top of your scalp. That should have roused you, but no. The jungle was simply licking you, licking the minerals from your sweat.

"The final chapter, Martin. You nearly wrote the final chapter, of a story no one would ever read. You nearly had me stuck with you. I want it. I want that taste of the jungle so much. I was touching it through you. It was touching me back. Then I pulled away. Just in time. I want to reclaim myself from the jungle, not have it reclaim me.

"I withdrew from you, came back to this river and lowered you into the current. The wet and the cold should have snapped you right back. You're stubborn, Martin. You held on in there. The balance I'm talking about isn't a matter of staying on your feet. You were doing well enough with that. It's a balance between two worlds. Keeping one foot in each, feeling the full weight of your body in every tread."

"Two worlds?" I wonder what they are. "The Amazon and the Pyrenees? Then and now? Life and the afterlife?"

"You're advancing. At least you don't offer dreams and reality as a choice anymore. Simply put, one world is time. It's a chronological world. The only logic most lives run by is chronologic. It has the ultimate truth at the heart of it: 'First we're born and then we die.' The rest of chronologic is a dreary passage from minute to minute.

"The other world is outside of time. A timeless world. Few people choose to live in this world because most don't realize they can. They catch sight of it though. For them it is composed of moments of wonder. Or moments of fear. Occasions when they can look back and say, 'My heart stood still.' Such snatches of life beyond the norm are viewed like glimpses from a speeding train. There seems no chance of taking them as your own, they just fly by like instant memories. Do you remember though how sometimes at stations, when two trains are stopped beside each other, passengers from one look out at the passengers in the other, then suddenly their train is moving. At least it seems to be for there is movement past their window and the other passengers are left behind. Then the last carriage is gone and the station reappears. It was the other train that moved and not their own.

"That's an illustration of how life lets us step from speeding trains. Step from time into the timeless, and the train of your life will still be there whenever you return. It's going nowhere without you."

"It felt so real though." The twin impressions are still there in my hand. "I was holding on to a shell, then found I was actually holding on to a rock, but they both felt like themselves. What's the physical link between these two worlds?"

"One is just as physical as the other. The vibrational nature is different, but that's just like tuning to the same radio station in different parts of the globe. You simply have to change your own frequency. The physical is a mode of perception. It is better to think in terms of energy, and that is universal whatever form it takes."

"Can you experience the two simultaneously?"

"Time and timeless at the same time, you mean?" Carlos asks. "Ha!"

"So that's a stupid question?"

"Not stupid. Simply funny. It takes time to come up with the right questions. That's what much of life's about, so don't worry. The answer? The truth about time is that it doesn't march on. It's always prepared to wait for you. And can you be in more than one timeless place at once? Why bother? There are no pressures of time. Better to give your full awareness to wherever you choose to be. Shifting awareness from one place to another is like living in a disco's strobe lighting. Fun for a while, then you get to see that much of the dance is composed of what you're missing."

"But you said I was getting stuck. That the Amazon had hold of me and wouldn't let go. You had to pull me back. So it seems that my life in time, my chronological life, was about to go on without me."

"It wouldn't have gone on." He turns his head to face me. "It would have waited forever."

"Time stands still?"

"That's the divine order of things. It's the essence of what we call God. It's the span of all the energy that we call human life. This eternal wait for full appreciation."

"Appreciation?"

"You remember the truth of the chronological world?"

" 'First we're born and then we die.' "

"That's it. It doesn't matter whether we live for a day or a hundred and twenty years. In eternity, length doesn't matter. We are all immortal. What is unique is the opportunity to watch ourselves blaze and die. Do you think God is dead? Never. He's incapable of it. Appreciation of death is special to human life. There's no need to pay attention in eternity. What goes around comes around, miss it once and the opportunity will come around again. Such is limbo, such is hell. In life, no moment repeats itself. Understand that, and you see the moment's value. Life is finite, so each moment has infinity wrapped inside it. Seeing that is enlightenment. Bringing awareness to the passage of life, that is enlightenment. Seeing the end within the beginning of everything, caring for that fragility of the life we all share, this is the way to eternal life. An eternal life that isn't a hell of repetition, but a life filled with awareness and appreciation."

"I was appreciating the Amazon."

"Nonsense. You succumbed to it. It was ravishing you. You were lost in the timeless before you had a sense of what time was about. You were in a loop, boy. The eternal loop of pleasured oblivion."

The tone of his voice as much as his words unnerves me. Some violent shiver passes up from the base of my spine to fly out through the crown of my head, and my whole body is left shaking.

"Come," Carlos says, and offers his hand to help me get to my feet. "Let's get into the sun and make you warm."

I take his hand, steady myself on my feet for a moment, then follow him along the thin line of path that stretches along this side of the river.

10

POOLSIDE
REFLECTIONS

Carlos's socks leave damp prints on the rocks, and I place the prints of my own bare feet on top of them. He stops at a point where a series of huge white boulders squeezes the river into a narrow force, then releases it into a broad expanse that is a pool with the relative stillness of a lake.

He bends to take off his wet socks, then unbuckles his trousers.

"Strip!" he orders. "Lay your clothes out on these rocks. They'll soon be dry."

I look up to check that we are hidden from the road that runs through the valley. We seem well sheltered. When I turn back to Carlos he is draping his trousers over hot stone. He turns back and laughs when he sees the expression on my face.

"My joke!" he says. "And worth it just to see you now. Is that amazement, envy, or wonder?"

"Did you steal it from a horse?"

He looks down to admire himself. I note there is no underwear among the clothes on the rocks, so he must tuck his penis down a trouser leg.

"No, it's all mine." He lifts it up to admire it, then lets it flop back down. "I can do nothing with it, of course. Its length can serve no one. But when I got the chance to reconstitute myself anew, I granted myself this endowment. What man of imagination wouldn't?"

He takes off his jacket, his waistcoat, his shirt, lays them all flat against rocks, then turns back to me.

"I'm in good shape, no?"

For someone his age, it's true. There's little flab, and a barrel chest that he takes a deep breath to expand as I study him.

"Fine," I say. "But why not come back in a twenty-year-old body, if you had the choice?"

"I brought back the body that had fallen apart. I'm simply me without the sickness. There was too much sexual energy for my present purposes, so I tacked it onto the length of my dick. Ha!" He lifts wide his arms and looks up toward the sun. "Go on, God. Do me justice. Render me stone to be a statue to myself."

He holds the pose so long and so still I begin to fear that the wish is working. Then he lowers his arms, rubs his hands together, and looks at me.

"Come, Martin. Don't be shy. Get naked and sit by me."

I can't say I'm comfortable, but I obey. Leaving my clothes and trainers spread out on rocks to dry, I go and sit beside him. He has settled in a place where the branches of an oak reach out to give us shade.

"And now, our story begins," he tells me. "You were in the Amazon just now. Take me there in story. Tell me of your arrival in the clearing. Make the telling as immediate as when you were in that river just now. Drench me with it."

And I try to do so.

But first I get stuck.

"There's a story in my head. A children's story. Somehow I can't think of anything else. I've got to start there."

"What story?"

"Jack and the Beanstalk."

"Ha!" Carlos slaps his hands against his naked thighs, a sound as loud as his funny half laugh. "Good. Go on. Tell me."

. . .

"You know the story. I don't want to tell it all. Just recall some of the main details, I suppose. Jack takes the family cow off to market. It's the only valuable possession they have, and he is persuaded to trade it for a handful of beans."

"His mother's warned him against doing anything so stupid," Carlos joins in.

"And now she despairs. Her son's an utter fool in her eyes. He could have had gold but he chose the beans. She throws them away and one of them sprouts. The stem thickens to the strength of a tree trunk and the green shoot soars up, up, up till it pierces the clouds. There's little for Jack to do but climb it.

"Up there the place is rarefied, but it's no more heaven than Buckingham Palace or the White House is paradise on Earth. It's a piece of immaculate real estate, with a castle that's home to a fearsome giant. To the giant, Jack is a morsel of food. To Jack, the giant is the owner of a goose that lays golden eggs. With the goose tucked under his arm he flees. The giant roars and sets off in pursuit. Jack leaps to the beanstalk and climbs back down, and before the giant can follow and bring slaughter to the earth, Jack grabs an ax and chops the beanstalk down."

. . .

I stop speaking. Then I realize it's for me to carry on. "That's all there is to say of the story."

"I remember extra details."

"Me too. Somehow they don't seem important just now."

"Then find the importance in the story as you've told it," Carlos advises.

I consider it for a while.

"We're all Jack," I suddenly realize. "Every one of our party that is sitting in a longboat, heading down the Ucayali River with the Amazon jungle ahead and all around us. Jack near the beginning of his story."

"So what's already happened? Where are you all in terms of this fairy tale?"

"We've gone against the normal advice of the world. All of us are struggling financially. We've taken what we had, and instead of investing it in gold we've paid good money for this journey to Peru. We chew coca leaves in the Andes and prepare to drink plant extracts in a jungle clearing. We've spurned the mineral world to invest in the vegetable. And ayahuasca, the mashed pulp of a jungle vine, is our beanstalk. It's going to lead us out of our world and up above the clouds."

"OK, Jack. You're heading up your ayahuasca beanstalk. What's going to come?"

I think it through. It takes a while to simplify the wild drama of my own story into a fairy tale.

"I'll find somewhere magnificent but dangerous, some-where I feel very small. Tucked in a corner of a dark place I'll discover a real treasure. My job is to grab it to my chest and bring it home. It won't be easy. All the forces up there will try to stop me. The only thing to do is run and run, never stop and never look back, come back down to Earth and chop that old vine down as quick as I can so disasters can't follow me. I'll never be able to go up that vine again, but then I won't need to. Though it nearly killed me I've brought back what I wanted. My home is perfect now."

"There you go," Carlos says. "Your nutshell. Do you think you can fit your story into it?"

"It fits," I say. And I'm almost crying as I sit there naked on a rock, in an oak tree's shade. The wonder and beauty of the fit astonishes me. "I've never seen fairy tales in this way before. It seems like a map that explains my life."

"Nobody likes to be told how to live. The adventure of life is in all the not-knowing, all the mistakes made for ourselves. So the lives of those who have gone before us are left as stories. They explain what's happened, not what's going to happen. Fairy tales are for children, but told by adults. They are old seeds planted in young lives. Do you know the storyteller's definition of innocence?"

I shake my head.

"Innocence is a story waiting to be understood. And now, Martin, it is time to hear yours."

Even now, as I write, I see how Carlos keeps setting me up for my story. Yet I'm reluctant to begin. There is so much more contentment in simply sitting and listening to the river as it passes by.

"You make me nervous," I confess.

"Is it me, or the story you have to tell?"

"You've been so critical of me. No matter how I start I expect you'll find fault."

"You started long ago, Martin. We're both locked in this story now. We have to stay till the end. Don't worry about me. I won't say a word. Tell the story to yourself. I'll just sit here, mind my own business, watch my clothes steam, and eavesdrop."

● ● ●

I do, in fact, know how to tell a story. Excuse me if instead I tell it as I told it then. Despite Carlos's pretense at only eavesdropping, his very presence shaped my tale. Incidents that seemed trivial were illuminated in my memory. I kept my eyes closed through much of the account, but when I opened them it was still the Amazon that I saw. I am even-tempered, but you'd have had no sense of that if you'd seen me. I imagine I trembled and shook like someone in the throes of a breakdown, my voice bursting with anger one moment then quivering in a whisper the next.

To tell a story of a journey is to relive it afresh. English explorers kept a stiff upper lip for sane reasons. In hostile territory a show of extreme emotion simply marks you out as prey. I had bottled my emotions in order to survive. Now Carlos was the genie who uncorked my bottle.

What follows is an impassioned account. I could have tamed it, but sometimes taming is akin to lying.

I have to be responsible. Don't expect picturesque travel writing designed to entice you to visit the place for yourself. I used to write like that for newspapers. No more.

Apocalypse Now wasn't made as an ad for the Vietnamese Tourist Board.

And this is no ad for the Amazon.

● ● ●

Forget ecotourism. Just forget it. It's clear as our little party steps from the longboat and sinks in mud that we're entering a war zone. Don Pedro climbs the bank and hands our passports over a wooden parapet to two soldiers with automatic rifles. They look from the passport photos to us—it's something to do—then wave us on with their rifle butts.

Choose damnation if we want. We mean nothing to them.

Keith's prepared for the worst. He wears a battered felt hat and holds a mud-brown umbrella above his head as a parasol. The sun beats down on the river as he sits in the shade and smiles, tilting the parasol to enjoy such sights as toucans flashing colors and screeching and laughing as they dart between the highest branches of trees on the riverbank.

The rest of us burn in the sun. What doesn't hit us directly bounces off the river surface and tries to get us from a different angle.

We'll get no better view of the jungle till we come out the other side of the ordeal. On the banks of the river the vegetable world of the Amazon grows and bends and winds to weave a blockage of the sky. Like the way a fetus gets to see humanity from inside the womb— that's the kind of view the jungle gives of itself when you're inside it.

But we're on the river, so we get to see the jungle in some perspective. We've already driven mud roads for hours in cars, and sped full-throttle downriver for hours more. Now we climb from the longboat and slide through more mud to two hollowed-out logs. Their outboard motors extend from long metal limbs so they can be raised above the rocks and vegetable debris in the shallower waters of a tributary. Don Pedro rides the foremost prow, calling directions to the stern as we steer the navigable route.

And then the boats can go no further.

Here's where you get some social commentary. The truth is, I'm delivering a privileged whine. I'm all fortitude at the time, flush with exploratory zeal, the reality of the situation yet to dawn. But in fact all I have to do is step from the boat into the muddy waters of this tributary and wade my way upstream. I wear a small backpack, but the larger cases and full provisions are loaded onto the backs of locals who stepped on board our craft from thatched villages along the way. We term these men hunters, their modest heights doubled by the size of our loads, and these are the jungle familiars. They surge ahead of us and out of sight.

I carry a staff, a smooth limb of wood about six feet high. It renders me magnificent in my own eyes. I bear it the way I imagine Moses bore his in parting the Red Sea. It gives me balance and majesty. I'm forging up the river like a man in a myth.

Don Pedro is more sprightly. His route through the waters seems a way of walking upon them, so often does he find a strip so shallow his ankles are barely covered. But there are times the waters reach to our chests. Among us is the wife of the foremost hunter; she has come with her two daughters. One daughter's head peers above the water as her feet tread the riverbed. The other is tiny and is dragged along in the flow as she holds on to her mother's skirt, kicking with her legs. The mother's hands are filled with provisions.

I sweep the girl into my arm and hoist her high, she in one hand and the staff for balance in the other.

Which reminds me of a joke.

What do you call a young maiden on the back of a court jester?

Virgin on the ridiculous.

But I'm doing my best and feeling proud. We near the site of our camp and the bank is suddenly strewn with rocks and pebbles. I set the girl down and she hurries away, searching the ground near her feet. She bends and picks something up, which she carries to me as a gift.

I hold out my hand and a tiny stone, with rounded edges and shining a bright coral pink, drops from her fingers into my palm.

She is four years old and already teaching me the supreme lesson of the jungle. Nothing is given, no debt can be owed, for the code of the jungle is exchange. A lift through the waters for the little girl, a stone for me. The past is canceled and life goes on.

And before we climb the bank to our clearing, let me describe another wonder.

I read before coming that the villages of the Amazonian jungle were the world's foremost malarial zones. No problem, reassured don Pedro. His clearing by a waterfall has no record of mosquitoes. It is a miraculously mosquito-free zone. Any that might turn up will be free of the malarial parasite, because there are no infected villagers in flying range for them to pick up the disease from. Take antimalarial precautions if we wish, but the medication will work against the effects of the ayahuasca. And besides, why bring medicine into the jungle, which with all its natural remedies is the largest pharmacy on Earth?

And so it is with some dismay that we find the promised order of events inverted as each person steps from the boat. For around the head of everyone, permanent companions for our river walk, is a swirling black halo. Dark and doom-filled clouds of insects.

Through all the jungle swelter, mosquitoes have detected and swarmed to the warmth of our blood.

A real-time buzz passes my ear. Mosquitoes in this part of France have some sense of insect etiquette. They don't bite in sunlit hours but wait to swarm at dusk. This is some rogue female, out to disturb the order of things.

I stop my tale, hold my breath, and wait. The creature lands on my right thigh. I wait for her to pincer in and attach herself to my skin, then strike. The blow is sharp and hard. I take my hand away and see the tiny corpse splattered against my flesh, then look across at Carlos.

He is staring across the river to the far bank. The break in my story, the slap of my hand against my thigh—none of it appears to affect him.

The appearance of a mosquito in France at this moment of my story set in Peru is no coincidence. I know that much. And I know that Carlos is causal to the creature's appearance in some way.

Maybe this is a kindness, keeping me in two worlds when I might otherwise be lost.

Maybe not.

I've never thought the matter of trust through, but now I reach a decision that needs no thinking.

I don't trust Carlos.

And suddenly the killing of the mosquito is like the slaughter of an army. I take a deep breath and feel the strength of a conqueror. The decision not to trust Carlos is a breakthrough.

Such a breakthrough that I find I am waiting for him to acknowledge it. He's adept at reading my mind, and this moment is worthy of comment. He doesn't want my trust, nor my distrust either. I know that much.

"Trust yourself."

He doesn't say as much, but somehow I hear those words in my head.

I'm no longer telling my story for him, hoping for the favor of his interest. I'm simply telling it.

I close my eyes and continue. I'm back on the riverbank in the Amazon, but tired of the old perspective. I'm moving faster, close to the ground. There's an eagerness to take in every detail. It's like I'm scampering with the senses of a jungle rat.

There's no story now. Rats don't tell stories. Just the drama of observations.

Up the path channeled in the mud bank, surefooted now and not slithering, for there's no time to lose, I pass through the outer ring of trees to enter the clearing.

I've slushed through peat bogs in Ireland and come across stone circles and the fallen stones of beehive houses. Driven across the sands of Saudi Arabia to where withered palms surround adobe houses crumbling back to desert. Felt the bite of the winds of the Gobi Desert blasting the air where palace walls once stood.

Looked at the sky through a broken dome on a hillside near Mount Ararat where a sultan kept his harem, the black tar of bat droppings now caking curved walls.

My travels have shown me the ruins of the world, but nothing as sad as this.

Some trees lie where they fell. Most were dragged clear, but others were used to make the buildings. There are no walls to the encampment, but there is a range of thatched roofs mounted on pillars. I know the history. The rectangular roof to the right formed the first and only building for the first groups that came. Then other roofs were woven from leaves and raised above the ground.

Tambos, small square roofs mounted over sleeping platforms, circle the clearing. This is the accommodation. I scurry through the vegetation that's already cloaking the clearing a thick green, stems bending around me as I run, down a mud path through a forest of ferns, and there is the shack of the squat shithouse with slugs a luminous green and white on its walls. Back now and up to a higher level and the tambos of the hunters. Down once again but pause for the view of the ceremonial house. Twenty feet in circumference, the roof is mounted on spans of trees, ribbed like the web of a vast Amazonian spider. And beyond it I see the party rise into the clearing for the first time.

The sky is black but without thunder, and the monsoon rains are like a storm at sea, for the world is composed of water. Rain forests have little to do with the earth, for the soil and nutrients wash away and the land is like a liquid. Trees grow close to support each other, vines grapple trunks to hold them in place and reach for the heavens themselves, and in the clearing I see that our party is lost. There is nothing to support them, nothing to hold them up. Rain pours down them like an outer skin that is melting into mud.

They have hopes, but the hopes belong to dreams. They have praise for all the human endeavor that thought it could build a village in the jungle, but witness the puniness of what remains. Paddle a dugout canoe against the current and you work hard just to stay still. Rest for a moment and you're swept away. Jungle builders need the same perseverance. It needs commitment every waking moment and no holidays near the city. This camp has had no visit for six months. The party arrives in a new home as it's being consumed by the vegetable world.

And among the party I spy myself, wading to the meager shelter of the second tambo. Keith heads for the same resting place, each tambo home to two people. He's drenched despite his parasol.

It's too late. For all my ratlike speed at viewing the camp, I can't reverse history. My assessment shows how wise it is to flee, but the chance has gone. The boats that brought us have chugged away, and can't be brought back till the appointed time some two weeks hence. My story is locked in the pattern of fate that will bring it to its conclusion.

Still low to the ground I surrender my legs and sweep like water through the camp. I halt by the riverside, and time compacts for the rains to cease and water to steam from the land. The sun casts its light on an expanse of beauty, a waterfall some twenty-five feet high and eighty feet across.

"*I once saw a man take stance in the center of the fall,*" don Pedro will tell us. "*A god of the waterfall who stretches protection toward us all. And the deep pool before him has the energy of a goddess. It is there for bathing but never for play. It is not for water sports and splashing. Treat the pool with reverence and it will restore you, lend you the energy you need.*"

The waterfall roars, and as I speak with eyes closed it reaches out to break a wave against me.

I rub the water from my eyes and open them. Carlos is staring at me. Knees tucked close against his chest most likely, for such is the tidal splash he caused. He has bombed into the river pool.

"Ha!" he shouts. "Too much respect can kill a man. Come into the river and play."

He turns his body, wheeling an arm through the top of the water, and gathers a wave that he sweeps from the river to break against my chest and face. I don't think but jump in, aiming to land by his head and tug him underwater. The jump is fueled by anger. I want to grab his silver hair and drag him down, make him gasp and choke. But as I reach out there is nothing to grab. I turn and he is behind me, and splashes me again.

"Come, Martin," he calls. "Admit it. What was the best part of your stay?"

"That waterfall," I answer. "The waterfall and the pool. Playing in the pool."

"Ha!" Carlos says, and leaps from the water as though gulping at the laugh and swallowing it down. He smiles as if happy.

"Good. You're learning your lesson."

"What lesson?"

"The pool did restore you. It freed you into the spirit of play. The lesson? You ignored the advice of the self-styled expert and trusted yourself to nature instead. The joy you felt was respect enough. Now you can give thanks."

"How?"

"You're in a river pool. Stand still and feel it wrap around you. It carries flotsam much bigger than you, so feel its strength yet remember its care. Know how well you are being treated. Appreciate and give thanks."

I bend my knees to lower my shoulders beneath the surface, stretch wide my arms, tilt back my head for my eyelids to filter the colors of sun and sky, and giving thanks is immediate and easy. Appreciation washes through me like a river, and leaks from my eyes as tears.

I have practiced anger, pain, hurt, and acceptance from my time in the Amazon. I have never practiced thankfulness.

And as I do, I sense my story is about to take on new colors.

11

WHERE
THE BEE SUCKS

"Please," Carlos says once we are both dressed, "Take me somewhere that is special to you."

An image of such a place comes to my mind at the instant of his request, even down to the detail of yellow lichen on its stonework.

"I know of a place. But there are others that are nearer."

"You think I am old and tired?" Carlos strides ahead, leaping over rocks to find a path that leads up to the road. He talks as he goes, loud enough for me to hear as I trail behind him. "Remember the boy who flew down Machu Picchu? That is the sort of vigor I have. It's you who will work up a sweat. Come on. We'll take the asphalt way. Pump up some speed. And if you don't mind we'll walk in silence. You are in midstory. This walk need be no interruption."

As I hurry in his wake I recognize that he has chosen the route even though I am the one who is supposed to know the destination. I decide to say nothing until he leads us astray,

when I will make a great point of calling him back and setting him on the right path.

The road is just wide enough for two cars, though few
have need to come this way. The rocks to our left are often
sheer, rising into hills. Wild thyme and rosemary grow in the
fissures to scent the air we walk through. To our right is a
drop to the river and the valley floor. I am still getting used
to this view, for it changed the previous winter, fierce rain-
storms charging the river so that it cut a fresh course through
acres of previously undivided meadow.

The slight gradient sees us heading uphill. To reach
Mont Canigou from my village you must first climb high.
Then the road plummets toward the broad river valley that
takes in the town of Prades, the home of Pablo Casals and
birthplace of Thomas Merton, before the land heaves into
high mountains.

The road winds to keep itself tucked against the hillside,
and spans narrow gullies with bridges to keep to a level. Carlos's speed is that of a professional roadwalker. His arms
should be held like chicken wings at his sides, thrashing at the
air as his buttocks swing. In fact he has the demeanor of someone strolling; one hand holds the wrist of the other behind his
back, and he turns his head to look about him as he goes. But
for the rapid flash of his shoes darting along the road there is
no way to see where his speed is coming from. I do indeed
break into a sweat, and have to run for short spurts to keep up.

I overtake him once as we cross a bridge, so as to divert
him up a grassy road into the hills. Thirty yards in I stoop to
focus his attention on a flower growing by the roadside.

Honoring the challenge of maintaining silence I don't
speak, and the flower looks so like its name there is no real

need to introduce it. Eighteen inches high, the dark and light petals of its flowers lift and droop to form the replica of a bee, many such replicas all clustered around the stem. One of the delights in these mountains in summer is discovering orchids, several with flowers patterned on other images from nature. This is the bee orchid.

Carlos stops and smiles appreciatively, but he's not to be fooled. I showed him the orchid for its rareness and beauty, but also for the chance to pause and rest. Accepting that the grassy road was merely a diversion, he turns back to the asphalt and races on.

· · ·

As the road turns and begins a much steeper ascent his pace slows. I'm so hoping for some sign of collapse in him that I don't realize his slowing is on my behalf. I expect him to sit on the bench that is set in the shade of ash trees, and I show off by not even looking aside at him as I march past.

That nimble yet casual trot of his brings him to my side in an instant. Taking my arm he coaxes me from the road and down a short earth path with grasses lush and waist-high along its sides.

He has found a spring. He cups his hands beneath the flow of water from the hillside, and they are soon full. He mimes for me to open my mouth, then pours the water down my throat. I gasp at it, not realizing how dry I have become. He laughs, a breathy laugh with no vocal sound, then reaches more water for me. I study his face before opening my mouth for it. Sweat is streaming down my forehead to make my eyes sting, but the skin of his face is dry. He fetches more water up to my mouth, his fingernails resting on my lower

lip as he pours, till he sees that I am full. Then he is on his
way again, and I am once more struggling up the road in
pursuit.

There is not far to go now. I let myself slow down a little,
so that he will be a good way in front of me at the point
where we are to take a track down into the valley on our left.
I look forward to calling him back.

He doesn't look back to check with me. The turning
comes and he takes it, heading straight down the track. By
the time I am on the track too and able to look down at
where he is going, I see him disappear left along a narrow
path through a patch of woodland.

He is precisely on course for my secret destination. I have
looked forward to the drama of introducing it to him. Now
that drama is gone. Saving a secret for Carlos is like introducing your own body to a surgeon, who already knows it
better than you ever will simply from scanning an X ray.

I find Carlos inside the ruin. Though it carries the name
of Saint Felicity and dates back to the tenth century, this
chapel has more of an eighteenth- or nineteenth-century resonance for me, the feeling of an era smug with its own
achievements so that romance could be found in the crum-
bled walls of earlier civilizations. Blocks of dark stone, their
edges weathered by centuries and softened by lichen, stand
solid though the timber roof of this ruin is long gone. The
walls squeeze in and the earthen floor rises for the place
where the altar once stood. Carlos is seated on a loosened
stone in the main body of the chapel. An arched window in
the apse points up toward the sky.

"A sacred space with walls and no ceiling," Carlos
observes. "Please, sit here and take me to a sacred space with

a ceiling and no walls. Take me to the ceremonial hut in your jungle. Speak to me of a ceremony."

I sit where he pats the earth. In front of me is a square of cut stone, presumably fallen from the jagged space where walls once met the roof. It is colored in yellow lichen.

I am tired and a little bewildered, but as I gaze up the dark stone walls and meet the blue of the sky above, a memory of a ceremony is triggered and I have no strength to hold it back.

"I have an intention going into the ceremony," I remember.

"A grand one?"

"In its way. I ask for ayahuasca to show me its majesty, show how we fit into the scheme of things, and how we can best promote the richness of life on Earth."

"It gave you these teachings?"

"I'll tell the story. We'll see."

It's possible for me to take ayahuasca and feel no effect. Fear of the process can put up internal blocks that even major hallucinogens find it hard to break through. This time I am certain at once that the medicine has engaged. A technique I sometimes practice of focusing on the center of my forehead, summoning any sense of fragmentation in myself to cohere around that point, calls the medicine into consciousness. This is a soft manner of focusing, related to stories of the opening of the third eye, and is really a broadening of vision that sees through forms to the energy that lies behind them.

The soft focus is on the ayahuasca, and through it to a broad and illuminated realm of experience. The first vision behind my closed eyes is of a structure formed of thin interlocking blue bars, enmeshing with others and expanding and swirling, like an animated viewing of my own DNA, the matrix of my being.

The sequence subdues into one of a single stalk colored yellow and black, reaching from where I lie far into the heavens. And the evening's paisley swirl of psychedelic patterns is composed of peacock eyes. When don Pedro squats beside me the peacock pattern glows bright on his white-clad rump.

And it is such open-eyed visions that form the main wonder of the evening. I am directed by the medicine to look to my left and watch for what will appear. Keith is lying there, and as I watch him I take the opportunity of sending love his way. As I do so a shape forms above him. One cell, composed of light as much as anything, the color of clear plastic, drifts into space, then others flood in to honeycomb against it. Soon the cells are cells no more but compose a whole being.

I counsel this being in directed thought that Keith merits its care and affection. It turns its head at my intrusion—a calm and slow maneuver—and studies me. Its eyes are rounded cones that have no single point of focus; they are more a composition of energy cells, each of which is a lens. It turns its attention back to the figure below it.

The creature is clearly a bee, but more like the eternal spirit of bee some seven feet in length. Keith struggles a little beneath it, and the bee waits for the moment when the man relaxes, then it lowers its legs to hold him still. I watch pulses of light drop from the creature to enter the head and body of Keith. The operation successful, it swings its head toward me and comes my way.

An effect I notice under ayahuasca is the power of yawns. Special effects in movies show the heads of young men bursting their bonds to transform into the heads of werewolves. These ayahuasca yawns possess some such transfiguring quality. They mount on top of each other, wrench the jaw impossibly wide, and the sense is of a new being breaking out of my skin.

I lose sight of the bee as it hovers above me, but offer it a series of these mighty yawns and the sharp taste of nectar drops onto my tongue. I swallow it down with my saliva. The bee appears to take a full impression of my body as it feeds me; then it moves on.

I rest awhile, then am prompted to rise and turn to look outside. The ground just outside the ceremonial hut is busy with tiny beings that are strokes of white light about half an inch tall. They swarm in a pattern of labor, streaming in and out of the hut as though carrying materials, and indeed a structure appears around the prone figure of Keith. It is like a mosquito net, formed into a square tent as rigidly as if it were held up by poles. As I watch this tent of light another being enters, its body again a foot longer than Keith's, again with the power to lower its legs and hold the man still as it injects material into him. This creature is not a bee but is encased in the armor of a shell—a seven-foot-long beetle.

Again this creature comes to me and the taste of nectar returns to my mouth. This is an evening of receiving nourishment, but the matrix that I took to be my DNA is also linked with visions of energy lines stretched across my whole field of vision. Largely green, they are a usual visionary experience of ayahuasca for me, something like following the tracery of veins inside some cosmic leaf. Some call this the web of life, and as I lie still it is clear to me that if this is a web I am simply one of its strands. Nourishment comes through the web to feed me, while in exchange some other force is siphoned out from me to supply the rest of the web.

"Thank you," Carlos says. His words tell me my tale is finished. Till then I have been sitting with my eyes closed, as though still lying in the aftermath of the experience. "That will do for now."

"That's all there is," I reply, resentful at such a dismissive reception of my tale.

"It's fine. What you say is beautiful and clearly true. I was hoping for something more though."

"A seven-foot bee isn't good enough? You want a swarm of fifty-foot dragonflies? You want me to invent?"

"I'm sorry. I didn't mean to hurt you. I didn't know you were doing your best. Let me applaud." He claps his hands a few times, then stands up. The irony is not lost on me. "Can we leave now?"

"Go home, you mean?"

"No. Just out of this ruin. I wanted to bring you to your special place. I thought it would help contain you, like a pool with pearls to dive for. You could take a deep breath and dive deep for the pearls from your stories, feeling safe here. This chapel is no use at all though. I want you safe and it makes you scared. Scared to profane it.

"You think Saint Felicity worried about being holy? Not on your life. You don't choose a life out here unless you're consumed by passion. Confront the passionate woman in Felicity and you'd be running home to mother.

"I'd say forget it, but you can't. A chapel's a chapel to you. It leaves you fractured. You divide yourself into good

119

and bad, and you try and show just the good part here. Good
and bad are like left and right, interchangeable according to
perspective, equal parts of an indivisible whole. You want the
world to be beautiful. You learned in the Amazon that
beauty can be savage and wild. These walls won't let you
release that fact. We must leave them behind."

I join him outside.

"I liked the silent walk," I tell him. "It's hot. I'm tired.
I'm not really in a storytelling mood."

"Do you think your mood is of significance?"

It obviously isn't. Not wishing to admit that, I say nothing.

"Moods foster lies. A story worth telling tells itself. If you
were truly tired you'd put up less resistance. Let's sit by the
river."

In fact, if I have any special place at all at this point it is
by the river. I had never taken time to sit in the chapel
before. Now that I have, I understand why my memory first
turned there. Carlos may have found his initiation into the
mysteries of life in the jungles of his childhood. My own
childhood found mysteries in lush woodland. The stories of
my native mythology all took me into the heart of the
woods—fairy tales in which young men tied food in bundles
on the end of sticks and ventured into the forest. The witch
who lives in her gingerbread house in a forest clearing never
frightened me as if she were an evil character. She magne-
tized me. She was someone I wanted to meet, even if our
meeting entailed her destruction.

The early saints of England all lived in places such as this
one of Saint Felicity. They set their lives against wilderness.
In time barons would own the land and dispense livings and
parishes to priests, but this institution that became the
Church of England was not my real heritage. The barons and

squires built palatial estates for themselves, and tucked into woodland in their grounds would be curious buildings known as follies. The follies were often given over to the use of resident hermits. These men and sometimes women who reflected the wildness of Christ in their lives, who found deeper communion with the woods than with human society, they are the spiritual ancestors of my imagination.

The passion of Saint Felicity doesn't scare me. I find it hard to trust a dispassionate saint. Carlos and I have walked down the path, marked by stones, that leads to the river, grass of a shadow-soaked green all around it, and we stand beneath a tree to look out over the water. I am thinking of Saint Felicity.

"Have you ever seen her?" he asks.

"No, but I do feel her presence."

"Only in the ceremonies, or at other times?"

"Here. Only here." Then I first suspect we are talking at cross-purposes. "Do you mean Saint Felicity?"

"Who knows? Perhaps they are one and the same. I'm asking about the lady of ayahuasca. You asked to be shown the majesty of ayahuasca. For an Englishman, majesty must mean a queen. I thought you wished to meet the reigning queen of the jungle."

"I'd already met her. That came before the jungle."

Trained in his curious art of storytelling, I pause and close my eyes to recall the encounter.

"This is in New Mexico. My first true encounter with ayahuasca, when I listen with the ears of a jungle floor and my body stretches like a vine. At first I am directed to look high into one corner of the room. I see twin and tiny lights there, and from these lights white forms begin to drape themselves down till they reach the floor. The drapes fall as though from two shoulders and merge into the body of a great being. Then before the head appears to identify itself I receive another prompting. The same command that saw me look up for the being's appearance now requires me to bend my head. It is no idle command, for it comes with an explanation. If I set eyes on the majesty of this being, I will become transfixed by her image. Such a visual experience requires my submission, and this is not the use she has for me. Save myself the sight and I spare myself the blandness of worshipping her, which I could otherwise not resist. Bowing my head and not looking up is all she asks of me for now.

"I do so, and sense her come across to be with me. This is enough, that I recognize and understand the embrace of her protection. She supports me, but lays no claims on me."

"I'm told ayahuasca is a jealous mistress," Carlos comments.

"Really? Is that so? It's what don Pedro told me. Once you are on the path of ayahuasca, no other path is tolerated. Try and leave it and you will fade to nothing, probably painfully so."

"Then you are lucky. You were not claimed."

"Blessed," I suddenly realize, then tune to the direction of Carlos's gaze. He is looking at the edge of the river.

Broad flat stones run from the land some way into the water, their tops dry and white launchpads for a squadron of damselflies. For many thousands of years these insects, fairly few in number, have found no need to evolve. Their bodies are tubes of iridescent blue that they lift and turn to shine in sunlit air, gossamer wings turning to target them at tiny insects that waft with the river's breeze. Meal accomplished, they land again and wait for the next prey.

But the stones also eddy the river into swirls of varying currents, and it is one such miniature whirlpool that holds Carlos's attention. A damselfly is caught there, spinning around.

I lean down and scoop her clear with my cupped hands, letting the water stream out through my fingers so her feet have purchase on my palm. She straightens herself, shakes her wings, and takes off.

"You have a story for me," Carlos prompts me. "It is not a direct memory, which is why I remind you. But it completes your encounter with the bee and the beetle, I think."

It's true. I recall for him a story told by Keith. It concerns the day before the ceremony. Keith told it to me in response to my account of seeing the giant insects hovering over his body. He did not see them at the time, but felt some strong presence. He appreciated the lessons it brought of the reciprocity in nature.

Down by the river, Keith, who carries skills from his profession's minute scrutiny of legal documents into his observations of the natural world, stoops by a small puddle of water. The edges of the water are clustered with bees, an inch and a half in length, merging the bright stripes of their bodies in shifting patterns as they pile above and around one another for the chance to suck at rare mineral deposits, a white crust left by the water's evaporation.

As Keith admires this play of nature, a hand reaches in and picks a bee from the crowd. The hunter's son Diego is showing off. Knowing the bee does not sting, presuming Keith does not know this, the boy makes a show of bravery. His daring act accomplished, he flicks the bee into the river's edge. Caught by the water, the insect flutters its wings but cannot get free.

Keith turns a verbal attack on the boy first of all. Till now the man has been silent, so a sudden flow of Spanish takes the lad by surprise. Only mosquitoes can be killed, Keith tells him. All other insect life is sacred.

He turns back to the river, steps in to rescue the bee, but as he does so observes a miracle of flight, the bee shifting such a surge of speed into its wings that they beat to lift it out of the river and into the air.

Back at the camp Keith is writing in his journal when some movement on the ground beside the tambo attracts his attention. Rains are pouring, a drop hitting the edge of a beetle with such force and weight that the insect topples. It has fallen off a crest of mud and is on its back, kicking its legs, its head submerged in water.

Keith reaches down and sets the creature to rights. Back on its legs, it ambles off.

And so, it seems, the visits of the giant spirit bee and beetle were not random acts of nature. They were returns of attention, the jungle's and nature's rule of exchange. What we give, so shall we receive.

I have an aptitude for fun and play, but I can be earnest and pompous too. Pleased with what I have articulated, I feel my perceptions deserve a period of silence at the very least.

Somehow Carlos keeps turning all my expectations on their heads.

"Ha!" he explodes.

Damselflies zip from the stones as Carlos skips across them to stand with the river coursing around him. Hands by his sides he faces the flow of water, then the hands slowly float up till his arms are horizontal, not held there but resting on energy. For maybe five minutes he stays there, then flaps the arms and shakes his body before coming back to join me on the riverbank.

"It's no good," he confesses. "What you say disturbs me and I can't let it go. I didn't expect such a thing. Didn't expect to be emotional."

He sits down. The natural care and precision of his movements is gone. Half of him sits on a stone, the other half on grass, the imbalance of his body a measure of what seems to be going on inside. He looks at the river as he speaks, and while tears don't mark his face I see his eyes are moist. His voice is lower and his speech a little more gradual to filter his emotion.

"I want to tell you not to be so fucking insensitive." He glances up at me, registers my shock, flashes a quick grin that passes as soon as it shows itself, then looks back at the river. "That's how angry I feel. You go crowing about being plugged into the web of life. You parade your revelations about nature's give-and-take. You're still wet behind the ears. Still primed with vitality. Just you wait. Ultimately, dear boy, when push comes to shove there's no give anymore. It's take take take till you're used up and dry. Till you're dust blowing over the Arizona desert.

"I envy you. I've pitied you before, but now I envy you. Make the most of it. By the time I'm gone, which is not long now, there will be not a shred of pity or envy. I must burn them off. Cremate them in this sun before the sun goes down. For now, while I feel these emotions, let me indulge them.

"Do you know my last connection to the web of life? Plugged into plastic tubes and machinery. IV drips, catheters, morphine injections, oxygen tanks—that's how we hold on till the end. It's pathetic. Undignified. You don't know how angry that makes a man.

"This give-and-take is on a scale way beyond your ability to conceive it. And why shouldn't it be? Your body's fairly young. It's bound to be the center of your universe. Take from one body, feed to another, it's all the same to nature. That's a truer reality. While you're juicy and productive you're kept going, at the expense of so much else. Then the juice turns sour and you're expendable.

"Your lesson from the ceremony is fine. I'm not criticizing it. Everything is exchange. We two, we're exchanging. You'll appreciate that later. But there's a lesson beyond that you're missing. Do good and you'll be done good by—do you really believe that?"

His tone doesn't need me to answer. This is my time for listening.

"It's sentimental bullshit. Stuff like that sees Christians come apart in jungles. Light attracts dark, like candles attract moths. Children walking suburban streets, proud of their new sneakers, shining with health and goodness, are snatched into cars by perverts. That's a return for goodness. Good doesn't only attract good, Martin. Evil craves a bite of it. You're a saint? You're martyred. You're Christ? You're crucified. The little community you care for is so outnumbered you're labeled an ethnic minority? You're all massacred.

"You're right. Do good, and there are forces of goodness to take care of you. I wouldn't be here now if there weren't some goodness in you. Nor would I be here if you weren't so damned ignorant and confused.

"That's your lesson. Shake off your ignorance. The visions you see on ayahuasca? That's life. Available to you always. Your friend Keith was alert to the needs of life around him. He received some reward. You were alert to his experience, you sent love and counseled affection, you received your reward. The lesson is alertness. It's the need to take action as a consequence of full consciousness. Keith's first act when the boy discards the bee? He attacks. What does he attack? The ignorance in the boy that lets him do evil.

"Do good. That's great. But don't do good and expect thanks. Where you find harm, expect a cause. Sure, assist the victim of a street attack, but don't get mugged yourself. Look after what's in front of you, but look out for what's behind you as well. Spirit bee waits till Keith relaxes to give him due care and attention. That's another lesson. Stop struggling, grow calm, and tune in to your intuitions. Take their direction. When they steer you out of harm's way, don't be blind to the favor. Look back and find the source of the harm. Study and learn so you can act in the future."

He's reached the end of a sentence, but he lapses into silence so suddenly it's as though he's interrupted himself.

"Carlos!" he cries, and slaps the flat of his hand against his forehead.

He shifts his seat to the stone so that he is neatly balanced again and looks at me with his explanation.

"You realize what I'm doing? I'm teaching again. Back to my old habits. You were once a teacher?"

I nod.

"Then you know how hard it is. You find an emotion and make it a passion. Use it to enflame others. In the position of one who knows, you don't let yourself know nothing. Your emotion holds a lesson just for you, if you go quiet and pay it attention. Instead you preach it as a lesson for everyone. It's why evangelists preach hatred and prejudice. Evangelists.

I despise them. And that is not my emotion speaking, it's my studied opinion. They claim to channel the word of God. A filthy, disgusting, dangerous, and puerile claim. God is silent care and attention, not putrid defamations of humanity. Fools cloak themselves in the garb of gods and strut as petty dictators. Too grand and proud to believe they have feelings, they read flushes of embarrassment as divine inspiration. Voices of terror and not of love, they preach their fears instead of face them. Stir people to hate what they already fear and you're empowered with many followers. Spokespeople for God make me sick."

True to his word, and with surprising elegance, he turns his head to the side and a stream of vomit flows from his mouth to the ground. It is colored the yellow of the morning eggs.

"That's better," he says, and pulls a mustard-yellow handkerchief from his pocket to dab at his mouth. "I feel purged. Do you practice vomiting? As soon as you feel yourself filled with bile, let it go. It's a good practice.

"Now if you don't mind I could do with some help. Find me a pebble, will you? Smooth and flat."

I search through the stones gathered along the river's edge, find one, and bring it back. He takes it, thanks me, and stands. Twisting his body, then freezing it in the posture of a Greek discus thrower, he spins around to send the stone skimming along the river. I watch and count as it skips over the surface.

"Wonderful," he announces, and grins. "I've never done so well. Even as a boy. Now help me again, Martin. You do the talking so I don't get to teach. I was feeling emotions now and didn't face them. Whatever disturbed me is still there. Part of what I've lost. Please go ordinary for a while.

Tell me of everyday life in the jungle. How you lived. What you ate. Speak of that boy Diego."

I look for a stone for myself and send it skimming. It manages three hops. Carlos's hopped seven times before skipping a little mud bluff and going out of sight.

"In the beginning is the rain," I say, and wait to see what follows.

12

THE GATHERING SWARM

In the beginning is the rain, and in the rains mosquitoes throng. Sun comes out to steam the land, and in the steam mosquitoes throng. In the dusk mosquitoes throng. In the night, in the day, in the sun, in the shade, in the camp, in the jungle, in the hills, on the river, mosquitoes throng.

The beginning and the end of this story is rain, and its punctuation is the hum and bite of mosquitoes.

We have tents made of gauze for protection from insects. Mosquitoes coat the exterior, reaching through with their proboscises. Lean close enough and they have you, sucking your blood into their bellies. Our all-natural organic insect repellent they treat like a salad course.

Equivalent to the presence of mosquitoes is the absence of don Pedro. His tambo is set apart from the hunters' and our own, and he keeps to the shade of that or the shadows of the jungle. His appearance, like a cat's, is mainly for food.

Essential to the success of the ayahuasca ceremonies is the diet. At its purest this would consist of hearts of palm and water. The Amazonian version we enjoy consists of a white river fish, grilled without adornment, with a side dish of grilled plantain. The fish, *boqui chicos*, is chosen on account of its selective diet, which consists of fruit that falls from trees into the river. The creature is therefore fruit made flesh, and the flesh is riddled with bones.

Once his fish is picked clean, don Pedro carries its skeleton to the river. No one can help him, for if an enemy gets hold of the bones from his plate the shaman's life is in danger. The danger is extreme when the shaman is on a special diet. Curses might be planted on the bones, and the bones buried.

To illustrate the fact, don Pedro tells a dinnertime story.

"I was visiting a village on the edge of the jungle. Not unlike the Shipibo village we visited together, communal houses of thatched roofs raised high above platforms. Sitting in such a house it is possible to reflect on advanced civilization and see how little our technology gives us. Here, though there is every evidence of extreme poverty, sustenance comes from the living earth and the air is made cool as it breezes through the shade.

"But on a sleeping mat in the house lies an eighteen-year-old girl, her long black hair soaked in her sweat, her mouth open and rigid as cries of pain pass up from her stomach.

"Seldom have I arrived in a place at a more dramatic moment, for as the sick girl cries another hollers, shouting to be released from the grip of the sick girl's father. This struggling girl is nine years old. The man beats her, using his forearm as a club, as women stand around and scream at the girl. 'Where are the bones?' they shout at her. 'Where have you buried the bones?'

"Few girls are born to resist such attack. When the man releases her she runs to the edge of the platform and drops to the ground, then crawls beneath the boards of the house's platform. The adults climb down and bend to watch her. Little by little the young girl's fingers scrabble away a square of dirt. One by one she picks out the bones, then crawls out to lay them at the father's feet.

"He stares without picking them up. The women reach arms under the platform, pointing toward a square adjacent to the one the girl has cleared.

"It seems the girl has done all she can. This other square of dirt is not her responsibility but the province of 'the other one.' The women know at once who this other one is. She is an older woman, a witch, to whom the girl is apprenticed. The child received her call in a dream, following the sound of her name till it led her deep into a forest. The sound mingled with a smell of meat, and that smell led her to the open fire in which the meat was sizzling. Her hunger strong, the child took the meat from the witch and chewed it and swallowed it down. It was delicious.

"The meat was human flesh. On eating it the child was transformed. An innocent no more, she had become a witch."

We ask if the story has a happy ending.

"The body of the eighteen-year-old shuddered and died. As a shaman I was welcomed by the mothers of all the daughters, to cure these children of possible witchhood. I worked hard, did probable good, and prospered somewhat. Life is a war with a series of battles. I see no happy ending."

At the close of the meal we carry our separate tin plates down to the river, and each stands some distance from the other as we wash them clean. Fish dart to gulp at the scraps. Monsoon rain sweeps down to give the plates a final rinse.

I tip back my head. Slap a mosquito on my cheek. Open

my mouth and taste the rain. It is a treat to drink water that is not filtered or boiled, for raindrops touch my tongue with sweetness. Otherwise the diet includes nothing sweet and nothing touched by salt. The ayahuasca brew is foul and bitter. Such variations in taste are almost welcome.

A calamity hits the austere purity of our intentions, whereby the combination of diet and fasting was to sustain us throughout the two weeks of our stay. A woman in our party, her body chemistry awry, starts a period she isn't expecting. Menstruation has a shamanic force of its own that no sorcery of don Pedro can keep at bay. He sees its energy swirl around the camp. For a while it seems the ceremonies must cease, but then only the woman is excluded.

Wiser than many, before coming to Peru she hung an Indian shawl over a clothesline at home. Bright red with patterning of yellow and orange, it is large enough to wrap a corpse. She sprayed it once with the most poisonous insect repellent available, let it dry, then sprayed it again. This she has brought with her to drape around herself, chain-smoking hand-rolled cigarettes to keep mosquitoes from the unprotected portions of her face. She looks like a woman in purdah, and now she is such a woman. Cross-legged on the platform in her tambo, holes burned in the gauze netting of her tent by her cigarettes, she sits bundled while smoke puffs and billows from her mouth.

Her menstruation, for some reason, has broken the diet of us all. Don Pedro leads the lamentation while jungle guinea pig roasts.

"One day's true diet is like ten years of spiritual practice," he explains. "Once I embarked on an eight-day diet in preparation for taking a new plant medicine. Just a little way into the diet I received a vision of a fleet of large, rich ships on a wide river. The captain appeared, walked up to me, and handed me his business card. 'All this will be yours,' he assured me, 'if you diet for eight years.'

"'I can't,'" I moaned.

"'Why not?' the captain asked. 'It's not so much to ask.'

"Then I realized that by eight years he meant eight days.

"Hunters in these jungles also diet. The diet is a cleansing and preparation to receive the wisdom of a plant medicine, and the diet is also the taking of the plant itself. When I speak of diet, I speak of all this. And for hunters, the diet is also their work. Honor this diet, and the prey is attracted to them while they track it down. The prey is attracted, the prey is tracked, the resolution is a meeting. Like the destiny of lovers.

"On one diet, the first two animals that come the hunters' way draw the fire of no shot or arrow. They must disappear in the way that they came, for these creatures are only phantasms. The third animal they see is ripe for the kill, for this creature is real."

The guinea pig oozes fat onto our plates. It comes with rice that is duly salted, and plantains that are sweet.

The way out of the diet is marked by a ceremony. Sitting on a stool in the ceremonial hut, don Pedro sings his enchantments and takes sips of Agua Florida, or "flavored water," which smells like cheap cologne. We each have our own bottle, individually empowered by the breath, songs, tobacco smoke, and sound of our names that a shaman passes into the liquid. This Agua Florida spurts as spray from the shaman's mouth to cleanse parts of the body; we take sips ourselves to spray over our chests, take a cigarette to puff smoke over our arms and legs and torso. With luck, with blessing, the smoke and the liquid dislodge the mosquito from her purchase on our skin. This ceremony is too profound for us to be swatting all the time.

The ceremony is completed with taking a spoonful of salt. The salt is fuel for tears of relief as we receive a meal worth enjoying. Then the diet resumes as we begin to purify ourselves once again, in preparation for the next ceremony.

Boqui chicos are almost as boring to catch as they are to eat. Gunshots ring out as hunters grasp the opportunity to track animals instead of fish. I am standing by the pool, setting my attempts at reflective stillness against the waterfall's roar, when a sound as loud as a gunshot breaks against a flat rock to my right. This is the sound made by a wet carcass of a deer falling twenty-five feet over a waterfall. A hunter hurries down a path to the side of the river and hauls the dead beast back into the water's flow, the easiest way of transporting it. Blood curls from its body to dilute in the river as the deer half bumps and half floats onto the rock that will be its final butchering site. Some of the animal will reach our tin plates. Most will travel on in boats to feed the hunters' families.

A small wooden boat is tethered to the bank just above the waterfall. I push off and sit in the bottom, dip the paddles in the water and set out to row as elegantly and effectively as I can. I forget that my rowing practice was not on a tributary of the Amazon but on small lakes in English parks, where it's required that you row round and round. I head upriver, but the bow of my boat veers toward the opposite bank and goes on veering. After some strenuous rowing the boat bumps into the bank just a few feet from my starting place.

I hear laughter. At first it is chuckles, then sidesplitting roll-on-the-floor hilarity. Diego the hunter's son is giving his hiding place away. Tracking members of our party is a favorite game of his. Best of all is tracking the women. They are much older than his mother, but they are forming the visions and fantasies of his dreams. Very best of all are those times in the morning and evening, when they wander down to the river to wash and he admires the white fullness of their breasts with their coating of soap. He loves each of the women in turn, and brings me reports of his passions.

Sometimes the women stay in the shelter of their tambos. At these times he tracks me. The youngest member of our party, I am the closest to being his playmate. As he peers out from the camouflage of the jungle, he cannot bear to stay hidden for long. I hear my name called, in a piping voice as soft as birdsong, and look to find his eager brown face smiling out from the leaves.

He picks himself up from his laughter and jumps into the boat, taking the paddles from my hands. Expertly he powers us up the river, and we duck the overhanging branches as we go. With the waterfall's roar left behind, this is my time for silent communion with the jungle.

It is Diego's time to sing. He sings of the Amazon. He sings of his love for Peru. He sings a song learned in school that contains the names of every South American country. And as he sings and smiles and paddles he teaches me the refrain, laughs at my memory and Spanish pronunciation, urges me to sing more loudly, and demands that I teach him a song of my own in return.

I sing him a song from a musical I have written. He is puzzled; the smile slips from his face. Then he sings his own Spanish song again, has me join in, and laughs with happiness.

Sometimes the boy turns into a man. He effects the transition by wiping all happiness from his features, for his impression of adults is of earnestness. Then, following his hunter father, he pads barefoot up the forest trails. A machete in hand, he helps clear the jungle trails. Visitors to the clearing are so few that soon after they are gone the jungle closes around the trails. Don Pedro's hope is for a steady stream of pilgrims on the ayahuasca trail. They will follow maintained paths to resting places in the hills of the jungle, and their money will help support a local economy in which hunters will once again learn to take a shaman's direction in managing resources.

It's a project doomed to failure on the acres of this reserve, for the shaman has lost the fundamental control over his tribe: his ability to command them to move on. An area can support people for only so long. Sustainability requires that they be seminomadic, but the jungle is now owned and there is nowhere to move to.

Back from clearing the trails, Diego is a thirteen-year-old boy again. He stands and lets the waterfall bounce off his head. Leaps into the pool with a child's delight and scream. Challenges me to race after race.

I explain that this pool is sacred, that it is not for racing or splashing but for reverence. Then I explain the fact again. After that, we race.

. . .

Keith has developed a technique for killing mosquitoes. It is his own version of hunting, using himself as bait.

"Let them dig in," he explains. And it is digging as much as puncturing. The creatures insert a sharp tube into the flesh, but the tube comes in two sections. First the bottom half pushes forward, then the top, shoveling ever deeper. The purpose of this tube is to inject saliva, which prevents the blood of its food from congealing on its passage into the creature's stomach. This is the way malarial parasites are injected into fresh organisms too. And it is this saliva that causes the irritation, swelling, and itching that accompany the bites.

Keith is being a true jungle hunter. He is attracting the prey as well as tracking it. And as is the case with any hunter in the jungle, he is also the prey himself.

His technique is precise: the timing is delicate. He aims to catch the mosquitoes while they are hooked into his skin, as they face a delay before they can extract themselves and dart away. But he intends also to catch them before they inject saliva into his system.

This hunting game is dicing with death. Both the insects' and his own. It's a version of Russian roulette. None of the mosquitoes might be loaded with the deadly malarial parasite. Or one of them might. The game is being played all over his exposed skin.

Maybe this is how tabla players in India establish their techniques. Swatting rhythms across their naked flesh, lightning speed to catch mosquitoes at dusk, learning how to strike their drums with the resonance of life and death.

"Got it!"

Keith slaps again, another tiny corpse splattered against his skin.

"And you, you bastard."

I look away from him, across the camp toward the cooking hut. This is a ceremonial day, so the aromas are not too enchanting. More *boqui chicos* and rubbery plantains to chew through. But the smell of the fire is always comforting, as is the glow of its embers and the lick of its flames around the water pot.

The fire is tended by Maria. She gathers the wood for its fuel too, and carries the water in pails from the river. She guts the fish and prepares the plantains. At breakfast, lunch, and dinnertime she is tirelessly at work to provide for us all.

In moments to herself she squats outside her tambo, spreads pieces of cloth over the surface of a sawn trunk, and uses a stick to mark in a design in mahogany dye. The maze-like pattern is learned and absorbed from her native Shipibo culture. The art is representational, a rendering of patterns observed in visions of ayahuasca. Women are traditionally kept from the plant medicine and the ceremonies, and this leaves them free to observe the practice on their own. These tender and expansive paintings are a feminine view, drawn from the source of the web of life.

Maria's husband was a famous ayahuasca shaman. They worked as a team, her role as a medicine woman being to prepare and help purge celebrants at the ceremony. Her study is the plants of the region, their roots and stems and leaves. She learned from apprenticeship, and lessons came from her own use of ayahuasca. She no longer imbibes this plant, for the rate of exchange is very high. It can take a high price for the lessons it gives. It took the life of her husband, for it is typical of shamans that while they are empowered to heal others they cannot heal themselves. And she knows that her own health might not survive one more encounter with the plant.

Bare-legged and barefoot, dressed in her wraparound black skirt bright with Shipibo design and her blouse of brightest green, her black hair tied to hang down her back, she treads the jungle paths to collect medicinal leaves. These are divided among plastic buckets and soaked in water, a daily gift for each of us in our party. Sun pushes into the mixture to heat and arouse it, blending the scents and juices from the leaves. And at a time of our choosing, generally just before sunset, we each step down and take a bucket for our ritual cleansing.

Facing the east first of all, the direction from where the sun gifts itself each day, we pour the first splashes of this plant bath over our heads. Then we face each of the other directions in turn, returning to the east in conclusion. The whole of our body is washed and scented. Scraps of green cling to our skin and our hair as we let ourselves dry in the air, sheltering in our tambos if the rain is falling, the juice of the plants feeding through our pores.

The night, closing in with a near-total blackness, witnesses sound replacing vision. Against the backdrop of a waterfall's roar, crickets call, monkeys shriek, and frogs croak and gurgle their liquid notes like the pulse of the jungle, like a marimba band. Piercing the night with a pencil torch you can find the frogs. Tiny as fingernails, sitting on leaves as broad as fields, puffing up their chests of glossy green, purple, or white, and singing.

. . .

"I'm growing mellow," I admit to don Pedro when we find we are near each other, both drying from our plant baths. "When I got here I was raging with anger. Angry with you, with the jungle, with the mosquitoes, with the rain. Now I find that is passing. I hate the mosquitoes still, but some calm is setting in."

"It's good," he says. "Good you are calm. But anger is good too. It's appropriate. The jungle is a place of great harmony. It is also a place where everything preys on something else. We prey and are preyed upon. Acceptance and alertness, calm and anger, that's a kind of harmony to see you through."

13

THE CARLOS
CONCERTO

You may have missed Carlos in the last chapter. Consider yourself lucky. The sequence and flow of my jungle reminiscences were pretty much as I have transcribed them here. That fact is one of the greater accomplishments of my speaking career.

"Go on," Carlos says, puzzled at my sudden silence.

"Do you want me to?"

"I asked you, didn't I?"

"But you're not listening. You keep running away while I'm speaking."

"You're still with me. So close you have no need to shout. So how is it that I am running away? I walk and listen, you walk and talk, we are still together. Go on."

So I do carry on with my tales and descriptions, but it's like walking a dog off the leash. A dog who trots across a room to the murmur of its name, but enjoys the sound rather than the content of heart-to-heart conversations. Though I am still in the broad consciousness of the creature, so that it turns its head occasionally to check out my where-abouts, I am quite subsidiary to its sense of freedom.

Carlos takes his direction from the river, but if he is now a dog he is no golden retriever. He doesn't enter the river for the fun of it, but only when it provides the simplest route. When rocks rise to cliffs on either side he takes off his shoes and socks, rolls up his trousers, and hurries through the water. Otherwise he keeps the river to his right-hand side and walks on the land.

Sometimes I think he is turning to me, about to com-ment on what I've said, but it's actually more like some pro-found nervous tic. His head snaps sideways to line up with his shoulder; then just as quickly he snaps it back to face for-ward again. He curls his fingers a little inward like an ape's, and stoops slightly as though his momentum is coming from the weight of his head.

I do my best to stay with him. His trousers give his legs protection while my legs are bare in shorts and are soon striped with the scratches of thorns, but though he once does look at my legs and their lines of blood it is with pass-ing interest. The only concern he shows is when I stop speak-ing. It takes him a few moments to register my silence, then he turns to me and spins a circle in the air with his hand. It is my continuity signal. I am to carry on.

There's no relation I can spot between what I am saying and what Carlos is doing. Perhaps he is undoing the previous enchantment, where I stepped from the bank of a French river and into the Amazon. Now I speak of the Amazon, while his attention is focused on the French landscape around him. It's as though I'm narrating the sound track to the wrong movie.

I try to justify Carlos's behavior. I recall how wrong it feels to step from a cinema matinee and find the world outside still bright with sunlight. I remember that Carlos is a master storyteller, and that stories belong to the darkness of night, conjured by the flames from a bonfire. I think how people dim the lights of an auditorium and make the surroundings sterile. Certainly I've never spoken to an audience that has been consumed with interest in the fabric of their seats, crawled down the aisles to investigate one another's footwear, fingered the bared weave in frayed carpeting, rubbed wet fingers around the brass plaques of seat numbers.

Such is my audience now. Carlos's body is a bag of sensations. He quivers with touch, sight, sound, smell, and taste. He pauses to stroke some grasses, nibbles a leaf from a branch and rolls it in the saliva of his mouth before swallowing it down, spins a pirouette to track the beating wings of a bird in flight, bulges eyes before the radiant turquoise of a scarab beetle clinging to the green of a stalk, and as we skirt a meadow he drops to his hands and knees and crawls fast with his nose to the ground.

I finish speaking as his body hangs poised above the ground, his nostrils snuffling up the spores from mulch beneath a beech tree. He makes no comment on the silence. I have no more to say in any case. I just sit in attendance while he scrabbles at the earth with his fingers, digging his way down.

He holds still, like an animal that freezes its prey before pouncing. Then digs in his right hand.

"Voilà!" he shouts.

He has pulled out a small black root, and holds it up in the nest of his fingers like a prize. Shuffling forward on his knees, he presents it to me.

"A man of my word," he announces. "I said I would find you food."

I study the root, sniff it, and sneeze. It's like the smell of being buried alive.

"What is it?"

"A truffle."

"What do I do with it?"

"You live in France and ask me what to do with a truffle? What's wrong with you? Filled with dreams and stories, have you no sense of where you are? Come with me."

He jumps to his feet. His nimbleness and enthusiasm are those of a man returned to his youth. I follow him, but when he stops it takes a while for me to reach his side. It's hot and I'm suddenly weary. I can't keep to the pace of this burst of living.

"Lie down," Carlos says, as though stepping back into empathy from his period of madness.

It's an easy command to follow, especially since he shows the way and lies down first.

"Close your eyes."

Tight as I close them, the sun still burns through my eyelids. My vision is a yellow dazzle.

"Hold your arm over your eyes."

That's better.

"Listen."

I wait for him to tell me something, but he says nothing. He must be listening too.

I concentrate, tuning in for the hum of distant conversation, the crack of a twig as someone approaches us along a path.

Still I hear nothing. Just the sound of the river. The constant rush of river water.

Water spilling over separate stones. A babble of sounds that stream into and around each other. The river runs, the strikes and beats of its music sustained in permanent echoes, sound mounting on sound to reach high and spread till it floods and washes the whole landscape.

Now I listen.

The valley is a canvas of sounds. The river is the under-coat and the final gloss. Other strokes sound between them till the canvas is filled.

The wings of a wood pigeon crack into flight. The rustle of leaves and creaking branch that it leaves. The tremble of birdsong across a hillside. The wind pouring sound through the echoes of river. The whisper of breeze from a mayfly's wings. The surging airward and snapping mouth of a trout. The swallowed silence of the mayfly. The thumping under-current of my heartbeat.

And the wind of a tune blown through Carlos's lips.

It is the seven-beat pulse song from the shaman in Peru. I hear it finding levels in the canvas of sound, laying mea-sures on the landscape.

Carlos repeats the tune, then goes quiet for a while. I am so habituated to the human voice that I take his quietness to be silence. He sings his tune in a different register and key each time. This is no arbitrary arrangement, but it takes a while before I see it.

A frog croaks.

There is a pause of several beats, then Carlos opens his throat. It is the frog who is conducting this section of song. Its croak sets the tone and the timing of Carlos's song.

Then I hear that there is no silence, simply a continuation of song. Carlos's voice is one instrument, perhaps an oboe, in an entire orchestra of sound. The frog is not ignored, but neither is it the sole conductor. It is one among a host of players whose notes add direction, harmonics, and rhythm.

Within this orchestra there is even a frog section. I focus on the frogs for a while, creatures lined along the river-source of sound. Their croaks syncopate around one another, pulsating notes of their scale, a dizzying excitement of noise that reaches a crescendo, sustains it, then suddenly stops. There is no diminuendo, no steady withdrawal of frogs from the chorus, simply one moment when they are all in full voice, the next when they have fallen silent.

Their silence is a sound, and they listen to it.

The notes played by boulders in the river, the percussion of crickets, the hum of insects drifting in and out of the foreground, the rustle of leaves, the high staccato of a red squirrel's cry—each joins the existing song and eases it toward a variation.

The song of Carlos picks from among this soundscape while my attention is elsewhere. Still keeping to a seven-beat principle, he extends his range to reach between a high falsetto and a cavernous rumble. Runs of notes quaver between the beats, music for a light-footed but energetic dance.

The song itself is a dance. I feel the tread of its notes across my body. They form a wave of delicate touch, like the trilling of a harpist's fingers, and I realize my body is being played. Carlos's song is stroking a song out of me. I don't feel tense, for the song of the landscape has subdued me, but I note a stiffness inside me.

I am holding my voice the way you hold a kite. To catch a wind you need to throw it high, but the kite stays rigid in your hand as you wait for the moment. Then up it goes. The string grows taut, the kite flies high, it is played by the wind but also by you. You keep a hold, keep control, while the kite expresses freedom.

My voice is now played like a kite. I let it go, but Carlos has control. It comes softly at first as I gauge its power. I sense the purpose of my singing, see that it brings the tread of Carlos's song from the surface of my body deep into its interior. My song is not an echo of Carlos's. It is more immediate. It is that song's reflection. When Carlos sings high, I sing high. When low, I sing low. For each of the dance steps in between my voice keeps pace, and our song is twinned. I am astonished at this ability to anticipate and chime with every instant variation; then astonishment moves to acceptance as my voice branches into variations of its own. They take the lead from Carlos, are tempered to match his song's flight, but from fueling his notes with my own sound they wheel away at times to add contrapuntal harmony.

I have ingested Carlos's song. I know the song is born from ayahuasca, for it takes the path of ayahuasca through my body. It explores, touches, and awakens every node. I feel a variation reach through my legs, traverse my feet, pump through each of my toes. I feel it surge in my chest, flow through my organs, shimmer along my arms. It touches my left cheek to leave it so clean I feel nothing but a hollow there, then moves around to wash my face away. Notes are sharp in the crown of my head, while a minor key stirs at my heart. My voice takes the song and adds vibrations, and my body vibrates as it hears its own song.

The song shifts. Carlos drops to a note so low I can't follow, a note that carries the color of blackness, a sustained resonance that shapes the image of a cave in my mind. The note is a resolution. I let the cave contain me, relax into silence, and lie still.

. . .

"Keep your eyes closed."

Carlos has rolled toward me to speak soft and direct in my ear.

"Let me guide you. Just a little way."

He takes my arm and helps me rise to my feet. We walk across the meadow grass. The sun's brightness dims. He turns me round and sits me down, then holds on to my shoulder and urges me back. I am resting against a tree.

"No hurry," he says. "Whenever you're ready you can open your eyes. You're in shade now. It won't hurt."

I keep my eyes closed and listen. The individual sounds, the river and winds, crickets and frogs, birdsong and stirring leaves, are still there. I no longer hear from inside them though.

"You feel tired. But it's not so."

This is a new game of Carlos's. Intuiting my emotions, then denying them.

"You think you have sung yourself dry. Again, it is not so. Your singing has recharged you."

I open my eyes. I have to do so before I can speak. With eyes closed my words would resonate inside me. I want a break from the intensity of that.

"It was beautiful," I admit.

Out in the meadow I can see the indentation left in the grass by my body.

"It continues," Carlos assures me. "Water evaporates, but it does not disappear. It simply takes another form. It is the same with your song. It still resounds. You can gather it in and resume it whenever you choose."

"Can I?" It seems doubtful to me. "When I first heard a shaman sing, I thought it was the voice of God. Or perhaps not the voice, but the direction. When don Pedro told me that twenty percent of the teachings of ayahuasca are true, the rest lies, it confirmed my experience. Teachings from ayahuasca come at me in five layers. Each layer seems true, but put them together and they are contradictory. It's like life in this media age. All truths are true, but some truths are truer than others.

"That's what the shaman's song shows me. When confused I listen, and one of the five truths resonates with the song. This is the truth to hold on to. Anchored to this truth I can go back and analyze the deception in the other four layers.

"Thanks for out there just now. You showed me the true nature of the shaman's song."

"You're paying me a compliment?"

"I'm thanking you."

"Well, don't. It's lazy."

"It's polite."

"Ha!" His snort of a laugh is dismissive. "I forget that you're English."

"You know where I grew up? The exact place?"

He goes silent and reflects.

"A little. It's coming. I'm getting a picture now that you ask me. Till now though it's hardly been current in your psyche. You've shut it off."

"What's the picture?"

"A tower. A redbrick tower with a parapet and a roof that's ocean green. Set in a parkland of English trees."

"That's the carillon. In Queen's Park in Loughborough. That's my hometown, in the heart of England. It's funny that's the image that comes to you. I never think of it at all. Now you mention it, I want to cry."

I hold back the tears, but explore the emotion.

"It must be a sacred space for me, the feeling is so strong. There are two duck ponds there. One has an island complete with a doll's house and is thick with trees and shrubs, where the ducks can roost in safety from foxes at night. The other tucks itself under a miniature bridge you can cross. There are twin aviaries with exotic birds, the screeches of peacocks on the lawns, flower beds rich with color. The town library is set alongside, and you can bring books out to the shade of trees and travel through their worlds. The carillon is a war memorial. The names of the dead are marked on plaques around its sides. It's a contrast to war, a peaceful place, a polite place. What's wrong with being polite?"

"Very clever. You have your own home in this media age. You build tracks with words. They lead away from things you're too uncomfortable to face. In my life, I was a gentleman. Now I have no interest in politeness. Politeness is not the subject.

151

"You thanked me for showing you the true nature of song. Am I to glow in your praise? Is your praise worth a fig? What is the true nature of song? You don't say. Is it an empty phrase? Some secret we share that can't be voiced?

"You are a writer, Martin. You have to work harder. If you've got the secret of the shaman's song, then deliver it."

"I was trying to!" I snap back, and catch the hint of a sob in my voice. I collect myself so I can sound more rational when I continue. "That's why I was bringing up Loughborough. You were on the mark when you saw the carillon. Walk up through its roof to its viewing platform and you pass through strutwork of heavy oak beams. From these beams hang a series of bells. The bells are made in Loughborough. There's a famous bell foundry there, Taylors. It even made the bells that hang in St. Paul's Cathedral.

"The carillon is different. The player strikes levers with his fists, and the bells ring out tunes. There are recitals in summer. But bells from Taylors also hang in the towers of churches throughout the county. Sometimes four, sometimes six, but best of all when there are eight bells. In the rest of Europe the bellringers ring out tunes, or simply toll the one bell. In Britain the peal from our church bells is unique. It's chain ringing, a folk art, bells wheeling through three hundred and sixty degrees. No tune, but a pattern of chimes, a gathering round in which each bell finds its slot with a mathematical precision.

"One of the most comforting mysteries of my childhood was the sound of these bells. I would lie in bed and listen to their patterns. The sound spread like a beam of light from a lighthouse, a similar rhythmical pattern combined with a sweep that brought it loud sometimes and faint at others.

"When I grew strong enough to hold the rope and not be hoisted to the rafters, I stood among the bellringers. The physical power I felt through the rope was immense. There was a thrill of power in myself too, that I could grip the rope and sustain the bell then release it in its swing once again, the clapper striking the metal and the tower resounding.

"But the magic was not in the individual bells. It was in their fusion. Whatever the round, whatever the pattern of strikes, the separate notes gathered inside the tower. The bells beat out a pulse but there was only one note, only one sound, the church tower filled with the single fused sound of all bells ringing. Separate bells ring out across the countryside, calling people to the church, and inside the church is held evidence of universal truth. For all the separate notes we strike, there is only one sound. For all our separate goals and ideals, there is only one truth. For all our idolatries out in the world, for every divine aspect and manifestation, there is only one God. Is that the nature of song?"

Carlos looks at me. "You say so much and still end with a question."

"OK. A statement. That is the nature of song. That is why the shaman's song showed me the direction of God. It was a song fueled by the spirit of a plant, a song in harmony with nature. I took it as an individual voice, but it was tuning itself to something greater. You sang with the frogs and the river, the birds and the trees and the wind, then I sang with you. We beat out our individual notes, but there was one sound. Find direction by that sound and we're steering by a universal truth."

"You think you've heard that sound?"

"Just now. You showed it me."

"The song of a valley? That's just one note. I'm talking about the sound."

I stare at him.

"You look so stupid, Martin. Happily you've done the homework. You've led a rich life. It's just that you're so dumb to it. It's time to walk you back through your own experience. Come with me. I have something to show you."

He steps out into the sunlight and meadow, and pauses by a flower. Its long stem of light green arcs toward its head of purest, brightest blue.

"It's very beautiful," I say. "This is what you have to show me?"

"This columbine? If only things were that simple. They could be. The columbine can teach you everything you need to know. But you're too locked in stories for that to work. Walk with me a little way further. We'll find what you need."

In the distance the river is spanned by the arches of a Roman bridge. Carlos sets his sights on it, and heads off.

14

THE SMELL
OF LOVE

Carlos walks in his nonchalant pose, hands clasped lightly behind his back, head turning to observe details of the countryside. At the same time he appears to be speeding, walking too fast away from me. My own movements are heavy, weighted with slow motion.

I want to shout at him to slow down, but I don't trust myself to come out with words. Whatever it is inside of me doesn't need a vocabulary to express itself.

It just wants to cry.

"See," Carlos says.

He has stopped short of the bridge and waited for me. He points to the ground.

It's a flower. Another orchid, its blooms the color of vanilla. They are not in the shape of bees, but are just as clearly distinguishable. Suspended from the stem of the orchid are figures of tiny men, with a head, arms, body, and legs composed of petals.

"It's grotesque," I say. My voice is an emotional growl.

"It's a flower."

"It sucks." I want to rip it out of the ground and smash it to pieces against a rock.

"Why don't you?"

"Are you reading my mind again?" I turn my anger on Carlos. "What is it with you? You lay me down to wash me in a world of beautiful sound. Then you force-march me through the sun to look at this filthy little thing."

"Why do you say it's filthy?"

"What are you now? My psychotherapist? Well, fuck off. I don't need one. Do you know what profession don Pedro had printed on his business card? Psychotherapist. Psychotherapy's not a profession. It's an obsession. Leave my psyche alone."

"This man-orchid makes you think of don Pedro?"

"It's a people-stick. I could see a jester running around with one of these and giggling. Jiggling these little people about in some crazy dance. Were they the English shamans? Our court jesters?"

"You think so?"

"I think so. That's what we do in England. Take what's dangerous and laugh at it."

"Shamans are dangerous?"

"When you go through life, good-humored and easygoing, ready to see the funny side, you don't recognize danger till it's too late."

"So where do you see the danger?"

"The danger's in a sound. The sound of someone having the last laugh. Not a ho-ho-ho kind of laugh. Some bitter, sardonic, triumphant snarl."

"Shamans have the last laugh?"

"It's the only laugh they allow themselves. Their only true laugh. Few get to hear it. They're usually done for by then."

I grasp the orchid with my fist. Earth scatters as I wrench it out of the ground. The petal figures of men go flying as I beat the flower against a stone. The stem and leaves are softened into pulp. I fling them away and rub my hands against a patch of grass, cleaning them of the green juice.

"Better now?" Carlos asks.

"You can't fool me. That was no innocent plant. It was poisonous. You poisoned it."

"I did?"

"I've never trusted you. And I was right."

He doesn't respond. As I wait I find my anger ebbing. I don't want it to go. I call it back.

"You're just like the others. Seduce me with something beautiful. That beautiful dream of sound back there was an illusion, I suppose? Then when you've got me all soft and opened up, you attack. That plant. You showed me it because you knew it was a symbol. It wasn't a flower anymore. You poisoned it with your intent. You wanted it to take me back to the jungle, to stir me up again. You and your fucking jungle. Well, it worked. Little people on a jiggle-stick, that's ayahuasca for you. We sip the brew of the vine and we're tacked on. You know what drinking ayahuasca's like? It's like plugging the umbilical cord back into your belly. You're back in that blissful mother stream, awake to the wonders and harmonies of nature. You're engaged once more in the flow of creation. The shaman plugs you in. Then he unplugs you."

"Sounds good to me."

"Do you want a suggestion for the world's most useless manual? 'How to startle a baby.' It's so easy. Shout at it. Frown at it. But there is a best of all. Rip it from its mother's breast while it's suckling. Go into the jungle, drink the shaman's brew, and you become a baby. A fetus. And the shaman is the midwife. Midwives, they're good things, right? But careless ones, selfish ones, they're abortionists too.

"That lady of ayahuasca? She's powerful, blissful, and real. But she has lousy attendants. I don't trust my God to the politicians of the Vatican. And I don't trust sacred plants to shamans.

"Let me tell you about me and my shaman. We're on a lake, our little boat accompanied by the leaps of freshwater dolphins. This is before the jungle. Don Pedro gives me a warning I fail to hear. Along the shore he has pointed out sites of his own early experiences with ayahuasca. Some of those shamans are working still, but he declares that he will not work with them again. There is not a single shaman that he would trust himself to, for they all have some agenda of their own. They all have some trick they wish to play with our consciousness, even if they believe it to be for our own good."

"They're all psychotherapists," Carlos says.

"Ha!" I respond, and am chilled by how like Carlos I sound. "I thought don Pedro was excluding himself. That he was the only shaman to trust. I was naive.

"He told us stories of attacks. How a shaman sets loose a dart that must be seen and diverted. It can be returned to the source, or sent to ricochet on its way, but once a dart is set loose it must find a target. In a similar way if a shaman sucks such poison from a victim, he must find a fresh victim to pass it on to. It is part of the jungle's code of exchange. To consent to leave one body, the poison must first be provided with another. There is no universal goodness in shamanism. Goodness for some is paid for by others. The sole concern of the shaman is what's good for him and his cohorts."

"And sometimes those he loves," Carlos suggests.

"I can't believe in a shaman's love."

"Then let me tell you a story. Once upon a time—"

"This is a fairy tale?"

"That's how I'm going to tell it."

Once upon a time in the land of Peru a man stepped out of the jungle. At his side but just two steps behind came his wife.

She was a child of the jungle. Her lineage on her mother's side stretched back to a woman we know as Eve, but the story passed down from mother to mother was different from the one that's in our books. In this mother's story Eve ate the fruit that we know as the apple, and thereby gained great knowledge. This knowledge came with a blessing and a curse.

The blessing? That the woman knew her birthright. The juice of the fruit passed down her throat and though it bore the taste of semen it had nothing to do with man. It was the surge of saplings out of raw earth, the bursting of blossom and swelling of fruit, the rotting of carcass and hum of a fly, the organics of death and perpetual birth. She knew herself to be seed and fruit, the place where death and birth both meet. Stroking her body she felt in touch with the presence of heaven on Earth.

The curse? That this knowledge could never be shared. It passed by right from woman to woman, but its light was too blind for man to behold.

The man we know as Adam clothed the body of his wife and dragged her from her realm. He could not rule in a fecund world. His paradise had to be sterile.

Our own story is contemporary. The man who comes out of the jungle with his wife two steps behind is a shaman. He wants to master a knowledge of his own. His wife is an intimate of the powers of life. He will choose to master death.

Incan lords never conquered the jungle. Their dominion was in the mountains. And it is to these mountains that the shaman now leads his wife. There is knowledge there that he needs to acquire. Knowledge of competition and death.

At night, in a chamber behind a locked door, he undresses his wife and lies with her. Her body is sleek, the sinews strong in the flesh of her limbs, and he lays his cheek on the sweat on her breasts. He smells the simmering milk of life, the steam that glues a jungle floor to its canopy of trees, passes his nose on down her body to sniff the spores that dance in jungle air, the scent of fish that tangle in jungle pools, and wets her body with his tears and the saliva from his mouth. This aroma of skin, her flavor on his tongue, is as close as he can come. Her smell is his strongest hint of her essence.

She has a primal beauty.

Born of the jungle, she has followed him to rock. There is no purchase for her here.

"She is weak and I am strong," the shaman feels, as disease clogs her heart. He tends her in the hospital

*ward of a high and dusty city, his nostrils filling with
the desiccation of death. He holds and caresses, washes
and dresses the body of his wife as she slides away to the
region of her ancestors.*

*"Oh yes!" she cries, in a passion she once expressed
for him. Her eyes are open, but she is seeing beyond this
world. Her ancestors are preparing a fiesta to welcome
her. They open wide their arms, ready to take her in
dance, and prepare themselves to sing the song that is
the happiness of her life.*

She dies.

*Two days pass. The shaman misses the wild taste
from her skin, the vital juice of her energy in his life. He
holds a cup to his lips, and tips ayahuasca down his
throat.*

*It is as though the ayahuasca carries eyes through
which he can see. Down the throat, down the tunnel, he
journeys into darkness. Deep within himself, deep
within the crust of the earth, it is the same thing. There
are creatures here, beasts the color of membrane that
move with the flip and blur of anxious flappings, eager
to greet him and grasp him and make him stay.*

*These are not the ancestors of his wife. He knows
that much. He seeks better company.*

*He hurries on, through tunnels and doors, a sequence
of empty chambers. He knows he is in the hallways of
death, but there is no wife to greet him. "Too soon," he
thinks. "I am here too soon, before she has had the
chance to reach here herself." The emptiness is desolate.*

*Then a tunnel ends in shadow, and he traces the
edges of darkness to reveal the shape of a man. Twice his
height and twice his breadth, swathed in a cloak that*

hoods its head. A draped arm stretches to the right. It is an invitation and a direction. The figure floats with the momentum of the arm, and the shaman follows behind.

The path is uphill, through a sequence of tunnels.

"Go," the figure says, and the voice is shaped from a stale gust of breath. "I can go no further. This is not your time and place. Go, and do not look back."

The tunnels branch through many doors, but through one door passes a scent the shaman remembers. It is the breeze, the steam, the memory of his wife. He opens that door and daylight touches the darkness of the passage. He follows the scent again. The door opens to a rose-colored pink, the hint of a distant dawn. Again, and there is a wash of light blue, the salted smell of ocean. Again, and there is a herald of spring as a breeze carries the fresh breath of grass. Again, and there is the moisture of cloud clinging to his body. It wraps him in a silver light and bears him back to life.

The journey ends. He has visited death and returned to the land of the living.

The lesson is clear. He entered the vision a widower, and returned a true shaman. He can now trade in his expertise, and deal in the realm of the dead.

Sometimes still he turns his head, catching the aroma of his wife. At others he hears it whistle as it blows past. It carries a secret just beyond his reach. The woman's secret of life.

"I'll find it out," he yells to her, though only he is listening. "I'll live till I've found your secret of life."

And that, as I understand it, is the story of one shaman's love.

"Is that your story?" I ask.

"I'm no shaman. It is the story of a man I care for."

I look at the flowers of the man-orchid that lie around me. With my finger I prop one up onto its feet. Then I take my finger away.

"Not much good, is it?" I say.

I try again. The figure falls again. I laugh, and stand up.

"The last laugh," Carlos observes.

I glare at him.

"You don't trust me. You don't trust don Pedro. There's no one to trust but yourself."

"That's right," I declare.

"Don Pedro, your friend, became your enemy."

"He nearly killed me."

"So you become your enemy."

I raise an eyebrow in query.

"It's a simple rule. I engaged with you. I became you. Engage with your friend, you become your friend. Engage with your enemy, you become your enemy. You're Martin, the shaman who survived."

"I'm no shaman."

"Ha!"

"No one died for my benefit."

"You suffered. You learned. Now you know better. Next time you can make someone suffer in your place." He looks at me and laughs. Not a last laugh. It's more of a blast from the belly, a ho-ho-ho. "Puzzled and angry and so very fierce. You're a picture, Martin. And what I say is true. You saw death and came back to life. It makes you a shaman. A creature of the jungle. You value life as you never have before. You'd sooner kill than be killed."

"Who wouldn't?"

"Ah-ha!" He licks a finger and holds it up in the air, as though testing the wind. "A good question."

He points the moist finger to beyond the bridge.

"Let's go down to the river and find the answer."

"The answer's down there?"

"Of course," he says, and laughs again as he starts to walk away. "The answer's always somewhere else."

15

A FISH ON DRY GROUND

"Do you remember your question?" Carlos asks.

We have passed the bridge and kept some feet back from the water. The hillsides are coated with scrub and brush, but trees of real substance line the river. It is under such trees that he asked me to stop and lie down.

"Who wouldn't rather kill than be killed?"

"Good. Now we shall wait for the answer. Keep your eyes open till you feel called to close them. Broaden your focus. See to the sides while you're looking straight up. And please speak. Remember, we are looking for a memory. We are looking for an answer. What do you see?"

"Sky."

"Just sky?"

"Trees."

"Whole trees?"

"Branches. Branches of trees."

"Are they still or are they moving?"

"Not still."

Leaves turn to catch light and shimmer against the sky. Whole boughs sway. It's a delicate motion, for the air in the valley is moving as a breeze rather than wind, but I watch the movement as a bough leans inward a little, then lifts away. Then I see that all the branches are moving in this way. It is soothing to watch them, like the calm I can absorb from watching waves ripple up a shore.

"Their limbs are moving," I say, and am surprised at a quiver of panic in my voice.

"Moving away, or moving in?"

"In. They're coming in. They're bending over me. Drawing closer."

The swaying of the branches is not violent, but dramatic. They sweep in, leaves swooping from distant specks to almost brush my eyelids.

"It's beginning, Martin." Carlos lays a hand over my eyes. I would expect a callused hand but the skin is smooth and cool. "Keep your eyes closed."

I hadn't realized I'd closed them. The sight of the branches has stayed constant. I open my eyes and look out onto the darkness of Carlos's palm. Close them again and there the trees are, the tips of their branches brushing my skin.

"Remember where you are."

I'm in France. Beside a river. I'm in the Amazon too. The trees above me are a flashback. I recall the scene, trees of a jungle reaching out in silhouette against the night. These though are French trees, bright with daylight, preparing themselves for their operation.

"Let them be," Carlos advises. "They're looking for your answer. It's inside you. You know what's happening?"

"My vision. We're replaying my first ayahuasca journey of the jungle. I lay on the floor of the ceremonial hut and it was like I was on an operating table. Trees were the surgeons, bending in like this, reaching down limbs to probe and examine me."

"Let it come, Martin. Allow the journey to return, and tell it as it happens."

"Can you see it too?"

"I see it. But I need to hear it. I need to feel the journey's vibrations in your voice. Go on, Martin. Go on."

Carlos kneels by my side, one hand still against my eyes, the other laid against my stomach.

"Here comes death," I say.

"Don't analyze. Just describe."

"Here comes death," I repeat, for it's the only term that fits. The vibration in my voice sets my body shivering. This is no mere replay of a scene I've viewed before. Then I was naive. Now the scenes are colored with the shadow of what is to come.

. . .

Death takes the shape of a cross, and though it comes with no perspective I know from its composition that it is life-size. Human skulls, face-out with their empty grins, form the breadth of the main pillar. Skulls mounted on skulls rise high, more skulls forming the crossbeam.

The tone of this ayahuasca journey is set.

My ears wake up.

From a distance, beyond the ceremonial hut, out across the clearing, I hear the buzz of a single mosquito. It is as loud as if already in my ear. I follow the weaving direction of her flight, hear her lock onto the wave of my body heat, listen as she propels herself in a direct course toward me.

My hand is ready. The insect comes within reach. My hand reaches up, and my fingers pluck her from the air. They squeeze the life from her. They flick her away.

My ears pick out the traces of more flights, more insects. My senses are a radar scanning the attack. The image of skulls set the alert. This is more than the usual, drab blood-quest of the insects. I need no experience of demons to recognize them. These insects are guided by a mind that is not their own. They carry weapons of destruction that serve them no purpose. They are creatures of demonic intent. Targeted at me.

My right hand is agile. It catches and flicks clear each assault as it comes in. Catch. Flick. Catch. Flick. Catch. Flick.

The wave of insects is gone. My hand moves on. It grabs hold of my left shoulder.

There is no clear sense of why I have to do this. Just the absolute knowledge that it has to be done. It is no casual clasping. I grip tight, my fingers reaching through the flesh for bone.

Keith breaks from his own trance, escapes from his own ayahuasca journey, to sit beside me. He is aware that something is happening, something beyond regular human powers of control.

"I must hold on," I tell him.

My task is so simple, and so hard. There is no rationale to what I am doing, only pain in my hand, pain in my shoulder. Common sense insists I let go.

Common sense did not bring me into the jungle. It is too late to pay it any regard now.

I hold on, and my grip becomes a battle. Forces set themselves against me. They are forces of pain, of emotion, of sight and of sound.

"This is stupid," comes some internal prompting. "You are hurting yourself. Let go. Let go."

My hold relaxes, then my grip tightens again.

"No need to tighten," comes further advice. "You have done as much as a man can do. You have held on long enough. Let go. Let go."

The muscles in my hand slacken, then grow rigid again.

"Look!" A voice alerts me to the ayahuasca matrix of color and green light as it stretches across the entire span of the hut. "At last. Your goal. What better destination can there be? You have arrived now. You need hold on no more. Let go. Let go."

And temptation is here. Beauty is here. Maybe I can let go after all.

"Shall I hold on?" I ask.

Others lie around the perimeter of the hut, enclosed in their own journeys, but something from among them finds the voice to answer. It comes as a rush of collective breath, a strong but voiceless affirmation.

I hold on.

Voices are constant, a barrage of sound. Some plead, some remonstrate, some come with the air of friendly advice, some with rebuke. Some shout in triumph. "You've done it! You've done it! Well done, Martin! Now let go!"

Lights flash. Sounds swell. Voices merge into one shout, the shout swells into a roar, full-throttle thunder that echoes and multiplies inside the chamber of the hut. I look for the sound of the shaman's song to find the direction of God.

There is no song. There is no shaman.

I don't know that I can do what is to be done. I am puny against this surrounding force. All I can do is carry on. If I win, I win. If I fail, I fail. But I will fail with my hand still clutching my shoulder.

The world is simply volume, simply sound. In the beginning was a word like this, some self-sustaining crash of destruction and creation, a roar that is wrapped around every shriek and whisper that might ever be uttered and that gathers it home.

Then it subdues to the sound of volcanoes bursting out of earthquaked ground.

To the peace beneath the crest of a tidal wave.

To the rage of a waterfall. To the marimba band of tree frogs. To the breath of Keith beside me.

"Is it over?" I ask.

"Yes."

"Is it over?" I ask again.

The breath of the group rushes around the hut's perimeter and delivers me an affirmative. I need assurance beside my own, but I need my own knowledge too. I am aware of the group experience. There are things others know that I do not. And things I have just encountered they cannot be aware of.

I stand, eyes closed. Keith stands too, and takes hold of my right elbow to guide me. I walk from the hut to the clearing beyond.

"Can I let go?"

"Sure," Keith says.

"Really?"

"Really."

I release my hold on my shoulder. My body bends. My mouth opens. Vomit shoots from me. It feels as clean as a liquid breath.

I open my eyes.

No eyes have ever opened onto greater beauty. I gaze beyond the clearing to the trees. Branches intertwine to fold the jungle between themselves. Ferns arch their lacy silhouettes. It is a vision of Eden. A sampling of life on Earth before the taint of man.

Keith leads me back to my mat on the earthen floor. I smile and sit with open eyes, but the work of my hands is not done. There are stings lodged within me. My fingers pinch hold of my flesh, grab and wriggle till each sting is pulled free, and flung away. There are no forces against me now. This is a simple matter of clearing. Pinch. Pull. Fling. Pinch. Pull. Fling.

A lady of white, her face a blank of whiteness, her robe and hair white too, appears and stands to my left. To my right the green matrix of life extends itself, and from the center of this luminous web a lady of green appears. She too stands at a distance, observing, too wary of the contamination within me to come too close.

Pinch. Pull. Fling. Pinch. Pull. Fling. I cast the stings out of the circle.

I now have a sense of what I am doing. It goes beyond sense, but then everything is far beyond sense. My body is the earth. In vomiting it clean, in pulling out stings, I am clearing it of pollution. I am healing the globe of environmental degradation.

Maria approaches, embers glowing in her long-stemmed pipe, and blows smoke over my hands. She holds my bottle of Agua Florida to my lips. I take a sip and spray it across my legs, my arms, my chest. I swallow a little down, and take a gulp of water too. The water is a wash of such sweetness. It is a taste from a spring in paradise, a taste of a world untarnished by man.

I lie back, content and ignorant. The lady of white, the lady of green observe from a distance.

I think I am cleansed. They know better. Shamanic darts must find a victim. I cannot simply flick my stings away.

"Well done, Martin," I tell myself.

And as I rest, the poison burrows inside me.

. . .

"Nice story," Carlos says. "Have you told it many times?"

My eyes are open, Carlos's hands removed. The branches above me are a summer display of leaf, pleasing patterns against the blue of the sky. I sit up.

"Just a few. Not like that though. I was seeing the visions again. Hearing the roar."

"You were reviewing the memory. That's very different. Sifting through the material. Looking for your answer. Do you have it?"

Who wouldn't rather kill than be killed . . . ?

"No," I admit.

"The whole cosmos roars for you with every sound ever to be uttered, and you can't even tease out an answer?"

"That's not what it was about."

"Of course it's not. It's about your drama."

"It's about not giving in," I respond. "That's what I get from it. It's a lesson in nonattachment. A subtle lesson. I was attached to gripping my shoulder. It was a stupid thing, but that was OK. We all have our goals, the things we have to do.

What we can't be attached to is our sense of reason that can argue us out of what is right. We can't be attached to the opinion of others. They say what we do is bad, they say what we do is great, it's immaterial. We do what we do as well as we can, that's all there is to it. You're a writer, Carlos. You've been praised to the skies and attacked as the devil. It's immaterial. You wrote what you had to write. That's how it is. That's what I learned."

"But you couldn't answer your question."

"The answer wasn't there."

"Think about it." Carlos stands up. "Call me when you're ready."

"Do you know the answer? Can't you help me?"

He walks away.

"Jesus," I venture. "He didn't attack the guards who came to arrest him. He let himself be crucified. He's someone who wouldn't rather kill than be killed."

Carlos keeps on walking.

"Martyrs. I tried to live as a Baha'i once. What really got to me though was their take on humility. It went too far. Their ultimate goal seemed to be to follow their leader, Baha'ullah, to martyrdom. I couldn't see life was about that."

He reaches the river and sits down, but doesn't look back.

"The Jains. They wear masks so as not to breathe in any insects. Sweep the ground before their feet to clear ants out of their path. They respect life. They wouldn't kill."

Carlos takes off his shoes and socks.

"Suicides," I try. "They kill themselves. Maybe they'd choose to be killed if they could."

"Enough, Martin!" He does not shout, but his tone is cutting. He stands in his bare feet, and turns to face me. "Who needs these thoughts? In the time I have left, do you think I care to debate philosophy? Your answer lies in your experience. Find it there."

"I left out a big part. I never told you why the shaman wasn't there when I needed him."

"Forget it. I've heard enough. I'm not interested in other people. Stop. Think. Tell me your answer, or don't speak to me again."

He steps from the bank and into the water, holding steady while it courses round his ankles, then treads deeper.

I stand and walk away. Carlos's shift into attack mode has left me too turbulent to sit still. I want solidity beneath my feet. Not grass, not meadow, not dry earth. Something you can stamp on and not leave a trace.

There are two choices. I can scramble up the bank to the asphalt road, but that seems too final. Once on that I'll simply march away.

The other choice is the bridge over the river.

This looks more slender than when it was built, around seventeen hundred years ago. The Romans would have laid deeper levels of paving to carry troops and horses across, walls would have guarded the bridge's flanks. Once more bulky than now, the bridge has shed its trappings. Four arches link to span the river, stones layered between them to skim the slimmest crossing from one bank to the other. This essence of the bridge is where its strength lies.

I march across it, not quite stamping my feet but wanting to. I feel more petulant than angry. Carlos's demand seems unreasonable: He's posed a question as a riddle, and I've never been any good at riddles. My attempts at a serious answer were brushed aside. If he doesn't want me to talk again, then I won't. But I'm damned if I'll simply walk away.

A mood comes over me sometimes that I never had a

hold on till one day driving across the Saudi Arabian desert toward Medina. I watched four twists of sand, miniature whirlwinds each no wider than tiptoes at the base and, at the top of a funnel, some twenty feet higher, the width of a man with outstretched arms. Not moving fast, for in the desert there's nowhere to rush to, they were just a density of spinning with wavering tops. The sight of them was the image of certain moments in my life, when some internal storm flails with a fury I can barely contain. There's little I can do when such moods are on me but wait till the whirlwind exhausts itself and tumbles as dust.

There's such a whirlwind now. Its driving fuel is petulance.

I turn on the bridge and glare down at Carlos. There's power in such looks of mine. They can make nice people stutter and back away. They need to be looking at me for it to work though, their eyes soft and engaged with mine. Carlos has his back bent and is paying me no regard at all. His hands, fingers spread, are poised above the water and his focus is set just between them.

A purple heron, largely white for all its name, sometimes patrols this section of river. Carlos's stance, his patience, his utter stillness, his attention remind me of that bird. The frown is smoothed from my face as I stand and watch.

The waters are so clear I can see the drama unfolding. Watch a clutch of five rainbow trout push out from inside the shadow of the bridge to nudge their snouts round sunlit pebbles. They are moving with the direction of the river, tangles of weed streaming alongside, controlling the water with their fins to move steadily.

Three of the fish are youngsters. Two are adults, one of these truly handsome in size. A young fish passes beneath Carlos's hands, nibbling around the man's feet, moving on.

Carlos remains intensely still. Then the adult, the long one, the fat one, follows in the youngster's wake.

I don't see the movement. There's no splash, just the thrashing of water around the trout's tail. Its body is secure within Carlos's hands.

No one can catch and hold a trout, not with bare hands, yet this is what Carlos has done. He raises his head. He has been aware of me all along. His gaze locks into mine and he holds it there, the fish secure in his hands. Then his shoulders jerk. The hands and fish stream out of the water. He lets go and the fish keeps on coming, silver drops streaking from its speckled skin, its mouth agape, flying full speed toward my face.

There's no time to think. Just react. I slap the fish as hard as I can. Its flesh is firm against my hand, waterdrops spittle my face, the fish skids against the dust of the bridge and lies flapping.

I turn back to Carlos, seeing what else he might throw my way.

He is watching me still. His hands in the river are closed around a trout. I get ready for the next assault, the new fish thrown my way, but Carlos simply stays still. I look at the fish in his hands. A long and fat fish. I look aside to the dust of the bridge.

The dust is dry. There is no fish there.

I know my experience. Carlos threw me a fish that I batted aside. But I know my current experience too. Carlos is holding the exact same fish in the river.

He turns his head away and finds a boulder rising out of the shallows. Still stooped he edges toward it, retaining his hold on the trout, and sits down.

A shiver collects near the space of my spine and shakes itself loose. My body shakes. I know the cause. It's revulsion.

I remember the face of the fish just before I struck it, recall the glaze of its eye, then shudder again. Watch in my memory as the creature bends and flexes against the ground and skids on to lie thrashing and gasping at the air.

I know what I did. I left it there and stood waiting to beat away the next one.

I retrace my steps across the bridge and walk down to the riverbank. Carlos looks up at me.

"Who wouldn't rather kill than be killed?"

I have my answer at last. It has come from my experience.

"Not me," I say.

He smiles.

"I have your dinner here," he says. "It's not for me. I shall not eat again. But you. There can be no finer dinner for you. Come here. Take it. Bash its brains out on this rock."

I shake my head.

"You mean you want me to let it go?"

I nod.

He opens his hands. The trout drifts forward in the current for a moment, then recognizes its freedom and spurts off.

Carlos stands and shuffles off to a tree that has fallen into the river, the torn clump of its roots lodged on the bank, and hoists himself up to perch on the trunk.

"Come," he says, and pats the space beside him. "Tell me about life while my feet dry."

. . .

"I love life," I tell him, and suddenly my body shakes with such a spasm I have to hold on to the tree so as not to fall off.

"You're shaking for joy?"

"Revulsion," I admit. "I'm sorry. I'd like to explain, but it's all a bit confusing."

"Let's do what you want to do then. Let's look at others. You looked for don Pedro's song in the ceremony but it wasn't there. Don Pedro had fled the hut. He had recently entrusted himself to work with another *curandero*, but things went wrong. Don Pedro's powers were drained from him, he found his colleague in sorcery was truly his rival, forces of destruction were worming between his internal organs, and now when he is on ayahuasca and at his most vulnerable a shamanic dart comes flying his way. He is alert enough to divert it, but knows that shamanic darts must lodge in a victim or they are still a threat to him. It's nothing personal. He wishes no one harm, but since someone must be injured it might as well be you. You're vulnerable, which is tempting in itself, you serve him no particular purpose, you're too naive to defend yourself, and you might just be strong enough to survive the attack. It's best for him to get out of harm's way though, just in case. If there's one shamanic dart, there might well be another. He can't go inflicting injury on everyone in his care."

"How do you know all this?"

"A friend of yours quizzed don Pedro in the wake of your illness. Don Pedro confessed the facts and your friend passed the news on to you."

"That's how I come to know it. But you . . ." I pause and reflect for a moment. "It's true, isn't it? You're plugged right into my memory bank. You know my experience as if it's your own."

"Yes that's true. Your recent experience especially. I've never hidden the fact."

"So why do you make me relive it all? Why do you have me tell all these stories?"

"Come now, Martin. Think of any conversation. Few people listen. They're just waiting for the chance to speak themselves. Conversation is much more about the need to speak than to listen."

"Maybe. But you've not gone to all this trouble just so I can parrot on."

"I want something from you. I want you to do something for me."

"What?"

"I'll tell you when you're ready."

"I'm ready now."

"You're getting there. I'll tell you soon. As part of our true conversation. I'm like everyone else. I'm waiting for my turn to speak. But first I'm giving everything I have to listening to you. That way you get to listen to yourself. When you've finished listening to yourself, you'll be ready."

"That fish . . . ," I say, changing tack rather than direction. "I saw it come flying at my face. I felt the weight of its body as I slapped it aside. But it never left the river. How did you do that?"

"What's a dream, Martin? Something thrown at you, or something you project yourself? You hate riddles. So here's one. What can you send that arrives without leaving you?"

"That fish?"

"A fax. But that fish is a good answer too. Who cares? It's only a riddle. Don't worry about what I do or don't do. Don't worry about anyone else. Look to yourself. Come on. You're getting there."

"I'm not. I'm lost."

"You say you love life."

"Yes. That's new. I used to go to bed at night and count the day another one ticked off. Life was OK but death was going to be sweeter. That changed. It changed when I saw such beauty in the jungle. That beauty was so physical, so voluptuous, it brought life so close. Breathe in and it's all inside me. Breathe out and I spill myself all over it. As close as that. I had a good aesthetic sense before that. I knew what I liked and why I liked it. This is different. It isn't appreciation at a distance. It's sensuous."

"The knowledge of Eve."

"You think? Maybe. It's not the knowledge of my mind, I know that much. It's the knowledge of my body. Carnal knowledge. A carnal love of the natural world. It's great, Carlos. It's new to me. I forget it much of the time, but when I remember to practice, it's such a thrill. It's my new religion."

"Not one you'd want to die for though."

"How could I? If my body dies my senses are gone. Then it's all over."

"Dying is sensual too."

"You enjoyed it?"

"Loathed it. It's sensual overkill. But sensual just the same."

"I went there, Carlos. Not all the way like you, but close enough. You know the details?"

"You want to trade hospital stories now?"

"No. Just tell you mine, I suppose. A plane brought me from the steam of the Amazon to New Mexico. It was like delivery from life in a lung. At home in the Sangre de Cristo Mountains near Santa Fe, way up at seven thousand five hundred feet, the air was dry and crystal clear. Nine weeks went by and I thought I was safe. Then an ache started in my shoulder.

Hours later malarial parasites stormed out of their incubation in my liver and took over my bloodstream. They gobbled up red cells and sent my body into its first spell of tremors.

"This was the deadly form of malaria. In the West we have pills that bring a cure. Pills we don't allow into the areas of disease so the parasites can't build up a resistance. Where the malaria is endemic thousands die. In the West we get to live. I take my pills, feel the malaria ebb, while the pain in my shoulder increases.

"To lift my head, to raise a finger, is agony. For weeks the pain is misdiagnosed. I crawl to the doctor on the way to the airport, looking for pain relief so I can return to England and free medical care. He tells me I won't survive the trip. I am ferried straight to hospital.

"There are X rays, there are CAT scans, there are MRI scans, I'm hooked to an IV drip, but as long as I'm still it doesn't matter what department they trolley me to. Completely motionless I'm fairly free of pain. With my eyes open I recognize the simplicity of death. It is simply one breath away. The choice is mine. Stop breathing, and it's all over.

"They analyze my illness. It is streptococcus, a bacterial infection of my blood. It started in my collarbone and spread down my left arm to my fingers, shifted down my chest to cluster round my heart. The location of the disease is what threw them off the scent. The combined experience of many doctors has never known the infection to take root around a collarbone. With the diagnosis in place they set to work. The attendant nurses take on the form of an ayahuasca vision, beings of light working to repair the damage of the jungle operations.

"Close my eyes instead of open them, take a breath instead of choosing to stop breathing, and I am taken out of my body. This is it, Carlos. I'm doing what you said. Listening to myself talk. I've felt no particular buzz till now, but this is something. This is what I've been leading up to.

"A skateboard is coming down a hill, three bowling balls taking a ride on it, the balls complete with the feathered headdresses and faces of comic-book Indians. Then they stop, and the balls become fissured rocks on the ground. In the melted features of one of them I recognize the nostrils of an Indian and travel inside it.

"I am in a tunnel now, composed of clouds shooting by in a blue sky, then beyond the clouds the tunnel continues through a long run of darkness.

"The destination is a place of equal darkness, but instead of the bounds of a tunnel there is a black plain I am standing on. A figure materializes in front of me. Composed of fibers of golden light, it is an old woman, bent toward me with her head hung low for her long hair to form a curtain between us. She moves her head and the hair, more fibers of light, begins to swing. I understand that this is my opportunity to make one wish.

"I can wish for the good of others. I can wish for peace. I can wish for health. Even for a place in heaven. The moment for the wish is there. It is the wish of an instant, with no room for moral contemplation.

"I state my wish.

"'Very much money,' I declare.

"The wish is gathered into the woman's hair and she flings her head to one side. The wish goes flying, caught by a naked golden youth of incredible beauty, and as he makes the catch this angel is transformed into a ball of light that soars toward the heavens.

"There you have it, Carlos. I go on a spiritual quest, am offered one wish from the gods, and I wish for money."

"Does it shame you?"

"I feel it should. But no. My life is fine. It lacks only money."

"You'd do good with it?"

"I think so. But who knows? The record of people using money well is not good. We'll see."

"You're sure the money will come?"

"Very much money. I'm certain. The wish was given to be granted." I turn to Carlos, and am smiling. "I'm not ashamed of my wish at all. I'm pleased at my presence of mind."

"Ha!" Carlos slaps his hands against his thighs. "This is better. The more unlikable you are, the more I like you. Goodman. That's your name. Is it right? Are you a good man?"

"I think so, yes."

"Ha ha ha ha ha!"

It's the fullest laughter I have ever known from him. He grabs hold of me to stop himself from slipping off the tree while his body rocks. His hands grip round my left shoulder.

I flinch.

His laughter stops.

"It still hurts?"

I'm in too much pain to speak, so simply nod.

"This is where the infection was?"

I nod again.

"And this is where you clutched yourself throughout that ceremony?"

I take deep breaths to steady myself and ease the pain before I speak.

"Exactly there."

"You should be dead," Carlos notes. "Something's looking after you. That's good or it's bad, who knows? The way of exchange is at work. You've been spared in order to do something."

"Aren't we all?"

"Ha!" The snort returns him to good humor. "Good point. People wonder where I learned so much. They search in esoteric places, rooting Indians and Mayans out of the hills. Do you know where I really learned so much? From the street kids of Rio and São Paolo. The most useless thing you can do in those streets is preach humility. Those kids survive where others would die. At least the survivors do. They're proud. They know they're as good as anyone. And they know the world treats them like shit. Humility's not where they're at. They've got to fight for their pride. Fight for each other. Fight fight fight.

"You say we're all spared in order to do something? Too right. So forget being grateful. Forget being humble. Life treats you like shit. It'll keep you in the gutter as long as it can. You've got to fight to get through it. Fight to do what you've got to do. Gripping your shoulder like you did? It's like a rat baring fangs at a coyote. On the face of it there's not a chance in hell. But if you're going to go out, go out fighting.

"Your question was fine. 'Who wouldn't rather kill than be killed?' you asked. 'Not me!' you answered. It's good. Why is it good?"

I can't think.

"I like you. I'll tell you. It's the only answer you could give. How can you answer for anyone else? You can, but you'd be fatuous. The best thing we can do to ourselves, the first thing we must do, is ask tough questions and face up to tough answers. What's your job in this world? Find your answer. Would you kill to stay alive? Find your answer. What would you fight for? These are the questions. Street questions. Give me more."

"How much shit am I prepared to take?"

"Not bad. And the answer?"

"No more."

"Give me another."

"What am I worth?"

"And the answer."

"More than anyone will give me till I screw them to the floor."

"This feel good?"

"Yes."

"So tell me about the revulsion."

I think of the fish, its face flying so close it seemed as big as mine.

"It wasn't the look of the fish," I say, and think on.

I remember the force with which I smashed it to one side.

"I didn't care about killing it. That feels bad, but it's not that."

I think on a little more.

"It's you." A shiver passes through my spine with the realization. "I was coming to trust you. Just a bit. Then you seemed to launch an attack. That made me sick. It revolted me. It shook me to my senses. I struck out. That's what it was."

"Kill or be killed. It's a rule of the jungle, a rule of life. I told you the story of the ayahuasca road. The shamans with their darts playing games on the side. Now take the story as your own. How does it play?"

"I went to Peru. Trekked into the Amazon. Joined the game without knowing the rules."

"Ignorant of the rules. The moves. The game plan. The players. Ignorant of the whole damned thing. You went in there primed with a New Age philosophy. You know what that philosophy is?"

I shake my head.

"Ignorance is bliss."

I have to laugh. "It's true," I concede. "I'd read about shamanic darts and all that, but I didn't believe in them. I thought they were part of superstition. Give the power of belief to superstitions and they exist. Otherwise they don't. It was a stupid thought, but it gave me comfort. The shamanic Amazon was don Pedro's world. I put myself in his care. I thought he would protect me from all I didn't understand."

"Were you ever a Boy Scout?"

"Yes."

"You were a lousy one. They've got a great motto. 'Be prepared.' You went to the jungle. You nearly died. Who takes the blame?"

"Don Pedro."

"You really think that?"

"Why not? He put himself forward as someone who could take care of me. He didn't. He nearly killed me. He'll kill others."

"Most likely. And you? Will you put yourself in his care again?"

"No way."

"Why not?"

"I've learned better."

"So you're no longer ignorant."

"I'm learning."

"You're growing up. Painfully, woefully slowly. Are you in my care now? Or are you wary?"

"Wary."

"Great. That's the way it should be. Come on. Let's continue our walk."

He nudges me to shift along the tree so he can climb down.

"So you're saying my ignorance is to blame?" I ask him.

"Ignorance brings lessons, not blame. Forget blame."

He slips his feet into his socks and dons his shoes.

"Where are we going?" I ask, for it's clear I'm not leading the way anymore.

He walks up to the bridge.

"You're wary," he announces with a grin. "But not wary enough. We're going to disturb you some more!"

16

THE SONG
OF YOUTH

"How do you tell when you're on the right path?" Carlos asks.

"Things go smoothly?"

"I said the right path, not a bland path. You know you're on the right path when things get interesting. But why am I running ahead? This is your adopted country. You lead."

The path bends to the right after crossing the river, before arcing left to go uphill. I pass Carlos and walk backwards for a moment, facing him as I introduce the way ahead.

"It's a Roman road. From around the third century." I've not taken the track very far before, but my years as a teacher leave me bluffing expertise at times. "We think of Roman roads as being straight, but not here. You'll see how the Pyrenees make everyone adapt. The road twists and turns."

I turn my attention back to the track. Turn and twist, leap and shout, stumble as I land and scamper up the track a few feet before facing Carlos again.

A snake lies between us. Its body, some five feet long and three inches wide, spans the path. My foot was about to step on it. I managed to hop and land beyond it, but my balance was gone.

"Cool," Carlos says.

It's not just hip appreciation. He's being descriptive in some way. Though it's baking in the sun the snake looks like it's fresh from the water. There is a sheen to its skin that shines the blend of turquoise and green of a Caribbean shore.

Two more things surprise me. The snake doesn't move and Carlos doesn't laugh at my clumsiness.

It seems my clumsiness is an irrelevance to Carlos, and that he isn't surprised at all. As I chatted to him about the Roman road he stepped more gently. I was going backwards at my regular pace and leaving him behind. The snake was hidden around a bend but he was already mindful of stepping into its presence.

"Stay where you are, Martin," he advises. "Don't move."

So far as I know such snakes aren't dangerous. At least not to me. Fishes and frogs should be wary. From my kitchen I sometimes see a curious wake cutting across the river, a snake's head breaking the surface as its body undulates to propel it. I feel awe rather than fear. But with the advice from Carlos, I freeze.

"Relax," he says. "The creature's safe. Just close your eyes and stay still."

I do as he says. I'm in sun, so rather than darkness there is the amber of sunlight through my eyelids. Then my body sheds some tension. It is as if some energy buzzing around my surface goes liquid and drops inside. The amber coloring before my eyes is still there, some external coating like the heat against my skin, but I sense another shade that is some-how tucked inside all of that. It feels like a cave, or perhaps the interior of a balloon, for it seems to expand as I rest in it. Its color is turquoise green.

"It's cool, yes?"

Carlos's voice is close. He has passed the snake to come up beside me.

And though I am standing in a blaze of sun I see the truth in what he is saying. The space I sense myself to be inside is cool.

"Welcome to the consciousness of our snake. Now please bid it goodbye and we shall move on."

"How do I do that?" And the other question I don't voice is, why do I do that? for this space seems most inviting.

"You are in the consciousness of the snake. It tolerates you but does not need you. Thank it for showing you a place of calm, and move on."

"Do I speak out loud?"

"The snake has felt your consciousness. I doubt it needs your language as well. But do what you will."

I thank the creature silently. It feels like a prayer. The sun startles me when I open my eyes.

"Take your time," Carlos says. "And might I suggest you now face the way you're going?"

· · ·

"That was a beautiful experience."

I'm setting a fast pace up the track, which vegetation has narrowed to a slither of path that in places is obscured com-pletely. The snake showed me a place of calm, but it has also excited me. I pant as I talk, Carlos tripping easily up the path behind me.

"There's a woman of ninety-four in the neighboring village. She wraps a red scarf around her head, knots it under
her chin, and heads out to work in her fields each day. She's
got a son, aged seventy-six, three times her size, with broad
shoulders and a strong back. I hear him, on his own, laugh
and joke. By her side he pinches his shoulders inwards and
looks down at the ground. I saw the two of them in their
field once. He was bending down to admire the beauty of a
grass snake. She ran up behind him and brought down the
side of her spade to chop the snake's head off, then smashed
the spade down again to batter its writhing body. She has
several of her own teeth still, and she hissed a laugh through
them. That's typical of these mountain villagers. There's
no such thing as an innocent snake in their eyes. Every
snake has to be killed. Many villagers have more venom than
a viper.

"Does everything have consciousness like that snake?
That's what you were doing when you were running like a
dog back there, wasn't it? Tuning in to the consciousness of
everything around you. Does this truffle you gave me have a
consciousness? Is that how you found it?"

I'm chattering so much I don't realize Carlos has
stopped. I carry on.

"That snake obviously sets up home wherever it is. My
home is what I own, I suppose, the place I put my things.
There's comfort inside its walls. Does the limit of human
consciousness of habitat come down to a sense of owner-
ship? There must be loads of other beings who treat our
homes as their own. The grass on our lawns. The dust mites.
Do dust mites have consciousness, Carlos?"

The response sounds like it could be his, some weird and
resounding grunt, but it comes from ahead on the path.

Branches of a shrub to my left crack and break, the bank of vegetation shakes, and a black figure snorts and heaves herself out onto the path, her front legs digging into the dirt and kicking up dust as she swings the bulk of her body round to face me.

She is eight feet further up the path. I stare into the nostrils of her pointed snout. They vibrate and spray snot to the sides. The nostrils stare at me while the creature's eyes hold me in black disregard.

She tenses and I expect her charge. A noise to her rear distracts her. I see nothing at first, then up the incline of the path scuttling young streak into view, squeals blown from their brown-striped watermelons of bodies, their trotters tearing at the ground.

The mother shifts her head to one side. I hear Carlos on the path behind me. The sow considers him, choosing whether to charge or disdain us, then hurls herself to the side. It's the first step in a maneuver that turns her round, exposes her flank, then launches her up the path in pursuit of her brood. The hoarse wailing of her grunts sees me stand still even when she is out of sight.

"Do dust mites have consciousness?" Carlos repeats for me. "Maybe as much as you, Martin. Maybe as much as you."

"Did you know she was there?"

"Breathe in."

I open my mouth and take a deep breath.

"No. Through your nose."

I do so.

"Again. And again."

"It's rich," I admit.

There's a scent of rosemary in the air from a bush to the

side the wild boar has all but destroyed in the heat of her escape, but the smell of the boar herself is far stronger.

"You indulge your powers, Martin. Powers like talking and tearing through the undergrowth. Yet you ignore the power of your senses."

"Are wild boars dangerous?"

"She's a mother. You cornered her with her babies. What's more dangerous than such a mother?"

"I used to argue there were still bears in these mountains. In cherry season I'd find these lumps of scat that were really clusters of cherry stones. They were in inaccessible places, on high terraces and along that narrow irrigation channel near my house, and I reckoned only bears could be so fruit-loving, big, and nimble. But the locals assure me the scat is of wild boars, who adore cherries. I've never seen one before, only heard them. It's funny they can be so fierce and threatening as that, yet have such delicate passions and skills."

"You should watch a jaguar kill someday. They can show the delicacy of a surgeon."

"Do you mind taking over the lead?" I ask.

Carlos smiles as he steps around me.

. . .

I was excited by the snake. I'm still more excited after the encounter with the wild boar. With Carlos up at the front it feels safe to keep on talking.

"This Roman road reminds me of a film I once made. It was about a Roman road even more buried than this one. There's a medieval house in the center of York, right next to the minster. Called the Treasurer's House, a beautiful place of oak beams and antiques. What interested me was its cellar.

York's the most haunted city in Europe, and this is the site of the most spectacular visitation.

"A plumber was working down there one day. In his off-duty hours he was a special constable, so his tale was to be believed. Working on some old piping, he suddenly heard the long blast of a horn, so loud and so close he dropped his tools and backed against the cellar wall. He stood quiet and stared as a Roman soldier appeared, complete in military tunic, shuffling steps of a tired march. Other soldiers followed, and horses with wounded soldiers draped across their backs. As he watched a whole brigade of Roman foot soldiers and cavalry march through the cellar, the plumber took in the details. Strangest of all was the fact that he never saw feet, not the feet of the soldiers or of the horses. These ghosts seemed to be walking on the stumps of legs, cut off below their knees.

"He said nothing at the time, fearing madness. Later, when a girl reported a similar visionary experience, he broke his silence to confirm the details of her report with his own. She too had heard the blast of a horn, and seen a footless troop march past.

"The matter was investigated. Historians searched through records, archaeologists dug through the flooring, and it was found that a Roman road had indeed passed through the site of the cellar. Only that road was a foot or more lower than the current level of the cellar floor. The Roman ghosts were marching along the road they once knew, their feet walking on the buried level of their memory."

"How did you film these ghosts?" Carlos asks.

"Mostly with sound effects and my own spoken narrative."

"So your film about Roman ghosts consists of you talking. Why am I not surprised?"

We have reached level ground so that our climb is over. Carlos steps from the path and sits down, patting the ground at his side. I sit down. Around us is a scattering of sun-bleached shells, the size of children's fingernails, the snails that once lived in them long gone. He picks up a few and drops them one at a time into my hand. He then picks up a stone, smooth and round and mottled pink, and adds it to the collection, before curling my fingers round into a loosely held fist.

"Please close your eyes again," he says.

When I've done so, he places his fingertips against my fist.

"What am I doing?" he asks.

"I don't know. I presume you're sending me into some kind of visionary state. I don't know how you do it though."

"Stay simple. What am I doing?"

"Touching my hand."

"How do you know that? Your eyes are closed."

"I can feel it."

"In your hand or in your brain?"

"Both, I suppose."

"And nerves buzz the message right through your system. You use your voice to pass the message on to me. My fingers brush against your hand, but in a very real way I'm touching your whole body. I can't touch your hand and not your body. Do you understand that?"

I nod my head.

"I'm being simple here. I want you to understand what is about to happen. This place you're sitting in the French Pyrenees. You feel it under your backside?"

The dry earth is covered with small stones that are digging into me. I wriggle a little.

"You feel it, and it feels you. And what is it, this spot in France? It's part of the whole Earth, just as your hand is a part of your body. Tell me, what's this?"

He touches my arm just above my wrist. I open my eyes to take a look. He's fingering a scar.

"I was taking the lid off a tin of paint in art class in school. Using a screwdriver. It slipped and gouged me just there."

"So it's a wound from a long time ago. But you can remember it and express it. I'm just skimming the surface of your capacity here. Compared to your body, any computer hard drive is like crude carving on stone. Every sound you've ever heard, every image you've ever seen, every sensation you've ever felt, every emotion that's ever swept through you, every thrill and every dullness, every delight and every pain, it's all stored somewhere in your body. You're a writer, you should know this. Everything is real. With so much to reassemble there's no need to invent. You just have to wake to the wonder and potential of experience. The moment of your conception is stored in you. It could take a lifetime just to express the fullness of that.

"Now imagine the earth. Four billion years of history if you can conceive of such nonsense of time. It's seen you rise out of it and it'll see you crumble back. It's felt its mountains rise and fall. Species evolved, then waned to extinction. Let's not even begin to think of the earth as part of something greater. Just reflect on this experience of billions of years. All that we can guess at, the infinite range of births and deaths and the dramas in between, the entire unknown history of life on Earth, is nothing more than the comings and goings of the pustules on skin. The greatest wars of our civilization? They rate with the eruption of an adolescent zit. We can walk, sail, ride and fly around the surface of the earth, mine it for gold and uncover uranium, but we never get close to penetrating its depths.

"That's a hint of the earth. We think of wisdom coming from experience. Imagine that kind of experience. Who needs access to more wisdom than that? I know you, Martin. You reach out for God and all the time he's under your butt. What is God? God is something bigger than you. You can look out into the cosmos but believe me the earth is big enough for one lifetime. Its wisdom is enough to direct you to wherever you need to go next. Are you ready to tune in to it?"

"The earth?"

"And all its experience. Are you daunted?"

"A little."

"Do you know what they say about a jungle-load of monkeys given enough time and encouragement among a forest of keyboards? They'll tap and tap till they've tapped out every word of Shakespeare. You know the funniest thing about that story? The achievement is more than Shakespeare could ever manage. He had a quill . . . and imagine that, imagine the primacy of writing with a sharpened feather . . . but not even a dream of a typewriter. Our technological era is so self-serving it sees even its trivia, its concept of a million manic typing monkeys, as the stuff of myth. Whoever Shakespeare was—and that might be a later conversation between us—he was surely a man who bridged city and country, who measured power play in the scope of seasons. He sensed the wisdom of the earth. And he was a writer.

"Do you know the difference between Shakespeare and a monkey? A writer and a scribbler?"

"Shakespeare was a genius."

"And the quality of genius? The ability to filter. The wisdom of the earth is a constant deluge. A genius lets through one piece at a time, and discovers its beauty. Then one more piece, and begins to build a pattern. Genius is the art of appreciating and reassembling the piecemeal beauty of the wisdom of the earth. That's a mouthful, but it sums it up.

"Now I have my request of you. You're a writer. A novelist. You know the immensity of tiny human details. You know a little, a microbial amount, about shamanism. You know a shaman cannot heal himself, only others. I ask you to heal me. I ask you to restore my boy Carlos."

His voice has been soft and measured. Now it bursts in volume, barely containing its passion. It feels like an accusation of theft.

"I can't just give him back. I've never seen your boy Carlos. I've not got him."

"You can find him. Bring him to me."

"Are we talking inner child here?"

"Cut the crap. We're talking youth, hope, vitality. We're talking jungle green, not desert dry. We're talking something you're able to do and are going to do. We're talking your life worth living."

"Are you threatening me?"

"You? You're nothing. You've got a future. Something you can be. You're threatening yourself if you don't follow me now. You tell me tired stories of exhausted Roman soldiers."

"It's a true story, so far as I know. A ghost story."

"And what am I? The air is stacked with memories. Hit replay and an image winds its way through. You step from time into the timeless and there's the same old loop playing itself out. You have me here and find interest in such stale reviewings? Ha!

"There are ghosts. There are ghouls. There are hallucinations. There are visions. It's the same in life as in the afterlife, if you'd only care to think about it. You learn the difference by sucking these encounters in. Feel emptied, sullied, disturbed, possessed, you haven't encountered a vision. Feel richer, broader, deeper, clearer, the vision and you are married. Now, marry me to the boy Carlos!"

"How?"

He grabs hold of my head and pulls it to him, pressing it side-on to his chest.

"Listen!"

I hear a rumble in his gut. Then the thump of his heartbeat.

He takes hold of my unclenched hand and places it flat against my own chest.

The resounding rhythm of his heart finds its echo inside me. My own heart was racing, but as I listen I feel its pace slow till it beats alongside the heart in Carlos's chest.

"There's your beat," he says. "Keep to it. Sit up."

He keeps my hand pressed over my chest as he raises me up.

"Your heart is under one hand. In the other, you are holding shells and a stone. Clutch them tight and they'll bring you back here, to whatever is now. Hold them loose, and they're the comfort of a soft baby's rattle. Please close your eyes. And open your mouth wide. Wider. Wider."

My face stretches into a chasm of a yawn.

"Your mouth and throat are filters. Your song is a siren call. Take the beat from your heart. Don't worry about words.

Shape the sounds as they come. Take your time. We're going timeless. No need to hurry. When you find your song lie back. It will keep on singing. You need only listen. Just listen. Sing, Martin. Sing."

I hear him settle on the ground to my side. Hear the breath inside my throat. Allow the first note, a staccato hum, to emerge. Range the same staccato hum up and down the octaves, scoping the possible limits of song so it will know where to sing for itself. Then start to listen as the song takes shape.

I expect the shape to be similar to the soundscape of earlier, when the whole valley became a composition in song. This song has a different intention. I hear nothing outside my head at first, the notes squeezed high to squeak around my cranium. Then less pressured, they explore the inside of my head. Notes become longer, my mouth opening and closing to round them, and lower as they gulp down my throat and reach around my heart. The song now swoops around my body, notes plunging ever deeper. The song claims my waist, moves down my legs, reaches my feet, and tucks around my toes. This weight of song collected in my body now leaves the body's confines for the first time. The notes go slightly lower, reaching below me into the earth. The song settles into the lowest note my voice can achieve, an open-throated bass growl that vibrates and builds and sinks still lower.

My song is now a single note, singing itself. I lay my back flat on the ground, stretch out my legs, and voice a final breath of the note as the song passes through me down into the ground.

I keep my hand against my heart and bring my other arm up to protect my eyes from sunlight. Following the song into the earth I expect darkness but already am catching glimpses of light. With my eyes shielded the journey gathers speed.

The light is green. Dark green, a merging of leaves, ferns, palm fronds, and shadows. There are times it rushes by as the green of the Amazon, times it takes on more light to be the green of Charnwood Forest from my childhood in England, jungle and woodland intermingling to form the walls, floor, and canopy around my propulsion. Then the rocketing speed slows and I am still. From the tunnel I have entered an expanse.

There is movement but no exertion. These new surroundings float toward and around me as I float within them. To my left I look up the long trunk of a palm tree whose fronds reach into a jungle canopy, while the light green leaves of a woodland oak brush my right cheek. The trees give way to stand behind me as I look down at my feet and see grass, look out and see an expanse of water.

The water is slate gray but shaded with the reflected hues of sky and cloud. It edges around a miniature island of tall grass and saplings. I know the setting. It is close to the English home of my youth. Across rolling fields, through gaps in hedges, across a high brick wall, through a stretch of overgrown woodland, this used to be a favorite destination. Beyond this lake rises a high hill, and on top of the hill is the redbrick expanse of an eighteenth-century mansion. I was trespassing yet also felt this land was private to me. I would take off my clothes, step through the mulch, and swim. It was a time of breaking bounds, so somehow also a time of freedom.

As I study the water I see it shiver. There is a ripple in reverse, waves sucked back into the center, and as the ripple disappears into stillness the surface of the lake is broken.

Silver light shimmers as a head emerges and flings water from its hair.

It is a boy.

He catches sight of me and smiles. I smile back as he swims a breaststroke toward the shore, the strokes bringing his shoulders up above the water. Then he stands, the water level dropping to close around his thighs, and steps up toward me.

He's smaller than me. Slimmer than me. As he climbs from the lake I see he moves with a vigor and grace that I lack. I guess he is about fourteen. The lake has washed his self-consciousness away. His naked skin glistens in the air.

I think he is smiling at me, but yet again he seems not to see me. As he comes close his steps don't shorten, his speed doesn't slacken. It seems confrontational but his face is so open, so happy, I don't move.

I feel the coolness of his skin when it has yet to touch me. Gaze back into the deep brown of his eyes. In the pupils of his eyes I catch my own reflection, and it is too late for surprise. I see my reflection, I see the boy, and I recognize that we are the same being. He opens his mouth as I open mine, there is a cry that passes between us, a mixture of sorrow and laughter that encompasses our name, and as he steps still closer and I feel his body merge into my own I see his face again.

And this time it is not my own young face. It has a similar tan of summer, a brown skin, but the hair is curled, the head is squarer, and the cry of his name is different. It's a fusion of sounds, one name layered on the other. I hear Martin. I hear Carlos. I catch reflections of my fourteen-year-old face as an alien boy steps inside me, feel joy as I and my fourteen-year-old self look out over our familiar lake, then look to one side at an unfamiliar expanse of jungle trailing roots and drooping branches into a river's edge.

"Cross your arms," I hear to my right. It is almost the voice of Carlos, the sonorous just-broken voice of an adolescent Carlos. "Hold yourself in."

I cross my arms across my chest and hold them there, sunlight now obliterating the jungle view as I sense a breeze against my face. The song of my journey continues. I hear its low sustained note, hear it throbbing higher, and sense it making its return journey: from me into the earth, and now from the earth up through the body of Carlos. It moves up through his chest as he sings, pipes through his throat, then mewls around his skull before fading into silence.

I turn my head to the side and open my eyes. Carlos is sitting with his back erect, his arms hugged tight around his chest. I sit up too, loosen my hold on the shells and stone, and shake them in my fist. They rattle quietly against each other.

Carlos turns his head to mine and opens his eyes. They are wet with tears.

"We thank you."

He shuffles around to face me, then unclasps his hug of himself, spreading his arms wide. The movement releases a force that folds around me.

"My boy Carlos and I thank you."

I let go of my handful of shells and stone and fling my own arms wide. Carlos reels back a little, enveloped by the energy my gesture releases. His response of openhearted laughter triggers my own.

. . .

"Stand up."

I get to my feet.

"Walk about."

The scattered snail shells splinter beneath the soles of my shoes. The baked ground feels like a professional racetrack, adding some spring in its surface to my step.

"Now you know what it's like to walk on the moon."

I take a few more steps, then laugh. I understand what Carlos means. I watched the first moon walk on black-and-white TV. All that science and technology so that man could learn to walk again, relayed with the amateurishness of a home movie. At the time I wondered what all the fuss was about, but now the image comes back with great tenderness. Those inflated space suits bouncing around, adult males sealed inside them, is a sublime comedy that I am also playing out. Some gravity is lifted as I walk, but my body feels as inert and bulging as those space suits. The new life that has slipped inside that body is taking it for a walk, and having fun with the experience.

Carlos jumps to his feet. It's a real accomplishment. I've known people to do it from a chair, a stool, a wall, but he springs upright from his seated posture on the ground and moves straight into the rhythm of a brisk walk.

"Time to go home," he announces, and heads across the high, burnt plain toward the scrub at its far edge.

"What's happening?" I call out as I follow.

"You feel good, no? Filled with energy?"

"Too good. Where's it come from?"

"You know who is talking? The old Martin. He's tired. Give him a rest. You've recaptured your youth. Enjoy it."

"Is it my youth, or yours? We seemed to get mixed up back there. I met the young version of me. But I met with you too, didn't I? I merged with the young Carlos."

"Youth is youth. The young are picky. They find one another attractive or unattractive. Grow old and the distinctions blur. All youth is attractive whatever form it takes."

He breaks from his route and trots off to the right. He pauses in the shade of a fig tree and reaches up. A fig lets go of the tree at the touch of his hand. By the time I reach him he has pulled back its skin. He presses the purple bud of fruit into my mouth. As I swallow he plucks three more figs from the tree and hands them to me.

"I never believed in the apple," he tells me. "Painters fix a fig leaf over the genitals of Adam and Eve. It's the sexiest leaf going. The curves of a body, the thickness of flesh, fibers you can stroke. What can be said for an apple leaf? Knowing that, compare the fruits. The fig is the real fruit of paradise. The fruit of temptation. Feed yourself as you walk. Keep yourself quiet."

"But—"

"But I want SILENCE!" He splays his hands wide and freezes his face in a grin, cocking his head as though listening to his shout disappear.

"There," he continues. "Silence. My wants come true. That's fine for me. What about you, Martin? Can you live with what you want?"

I know what I want. I want answers. I mean to get them. Whether I can live with them or not.

In the meantime I live with the silence as we walk.

17

CAVE
DWELLING

Carlos turns around. One moment he is leading the way in front of me, the next he is aiming directly at me. It is as though I'm not there.

He doesn't falter. I jump to the side the moment before we collide. He walks on, retracing our steps. Back across the plain. Switching down the Roman track to descend the hillside. Pacing over the bridge. Climbing up to the asphalt road and assuming a speed that makes me jog to catch up.

Heading back toward the village, he suddenly leaves the road and rips through undergrowth as he scrambles down the bank. I'd say he was running away from me, but he never looks back. A fleeing man keeps an eye on his pursuer. For Carlos I'm no longer there.

It's not just me who has slipped from his awareness. Even in his wildest moments, when the sensual stream of nature made him seem mad but never dizzy, he didn't stumble. Now I watch his arms flail, catching at balance as he trips on a rock. He sets foot in the river with the confidence of a man who walks on water, yet falls forward as a pebble turns beneath his foot. His body is fully submerged for a moment, then his arms wheel round like championship strokes of a butterfly swimmer and he surges up and forward with no loss in momentum.

I follow, but I don't even try to keep up.

Carlos is an old man, one who has befriended me, who is now clearly deranged and in need of help. Once out of the wood he tears through chest-high undergrowth, reaches out his left hand to curl around the trunk of a tree, veers forward and right to swing round the next, and disappears from sight but not from sound as he crashes onward.

I don't call out to him. I don't risk my own footing in pursuit. I check the river for a shallower crossing downstream, bother to take off my trainers so as to wade carefully across, listen for Carlos's progress as I put them on again and tie the laces, then don't even hurry as I make my way through the brief strip of woodland.

By the time I enter the meadow Carlos has already hurried across it and reached the red dirt of the hillside that sweeps up a curve into an almost vertical rise. He reaches for hand- and toeholds and hauls himself up to twice his own height before disappearing across the lower rim of a small, round cave.

· · ·

I pull myself up to look inside the cave. Carlos is sitting against the wall, bent forward slightly as the cave curves toward its ceiling. His legs stick straight out in front of him, his arms are wide to his sides with their palms flat against the rock. All is dark at first, then I adjust to the interior space and a rosy light picks out the features. It shows me Carlos's eyes. The eyelids are open but the pupils have rolled inside the head somewhere. It is the whites of his eyes that stare back at me.

There's room inside for me to climb up and join him. Just about.

Instead I drop down to the grass that runs up to the sharp edge of the hill and sit there. I give my thoughts time to settle, and they refuse. They have their own white-eyed focus, careering everywhere and finding no moment of sense. Maybe some physical movement will help coordinate me. I stand up and start to move away.

"Boy!"

The shout comes from the cave. With more strength of my own I would ignore it and keep on walking.

I go back.

• • •

Careful maneuvering inside the cave lets me slot into the available space. Carlos and I are at a slight angle to each other. It is as easy to look out over the landscape we have just walked as to look at each other. I study the view for a while before turning to face Carlos. His posture has not changed. As I reaccustom myself to the light of the cave I note that his eyes still glare white. Then the eyelids close, screw tight a moment, and snap open. He is staring at me.

His tone makes his first words an accusation. "What are you doing here?"

"You called me."

"Nonsense." He turns his head to face the view, then turns back to me again. "How did I call you?"

"Boy. You shouted Boy."

"Ha!" This is one of those snorts with no laughter in it. "You know why I ran just now? I was running away from you. Why should I call you? Is your name Boy? Do you see yourself as a boy and not a man?"

I say nothing.

"I'm more than you can handle. On my own, dry as dust, it was OK. With my boy Carlos in me it was different. I was an energy field that could burn you up. I ran away for your own good. Before you were cinders."

"You got your boy back and didn't need me anymore. That's the truth of it."

"You speak of truth? Show it to me. Go on. Point it out so I can take a look at it. Don't speak of truth again till you can do that much."

"You're the master of truth, I suppose. You can pull truth out of a pocket or from up your sleeve . . ." My words dry up. It feels good to be bickering with Carlos on equal terms. Then I notice I haven't risen to his level at all. Carlos has simply dropped to mine. A tear brims from his left eye and runs down his cheek. "You're crying."

"Stop interpreting. You see a tear. It doesn't mean I'm crying."

"What are you doing, then?"

"Are you mad? I'm dead. How can I be doing anything?"

"So what's the tear?"

"Moisture escaping dust. A trickling of sap. The last of my boy Carlos." His hands are still pressed against the walls. He brings his right one to his face and wipes the tear away. "There. I'm back to my dry old self."

"Maybe you want to be on your own?"

"You've got questions. You want answers. We might as well play this game to its conclusion."

"Is there a conclusion?"

"Everyone has a book in them. Almost none of them are writers, but that's not the point. It helps to think of life as a book with a great ending. When all seems mad, when there's no point carrying on, depression's weighty and suicide's the best way out, you have to trust in the greatness of your own book and hang in there. Tragedies do somersaults, crazy subplots stream together, redundant characters take curtain calls, loose ends get tied like satin bows, and all you can do if the pain's not too much is laugh at so much perfection."

"You're not laughing now."

"You're interpreting again. You hear no laughter and presume I'm not laughing. You're wrong. This is the most hilarious moment of my whole resurrection."

I wait for more, but it doesn't come.

"Sorry," I say. "I don't get the joke."

"That makes me feel better. I see a joke that you can't see. It's proof of my own existence."

"What's the joke?"

"Is this your first question? I've decided to allow you ten, starting now."

"Ten questions? Is a joke worth a question?"

"That's a question. A wasted one. My answer is yes. The nature of this joke is surely worth a question. You've got nine questions left."

"That's not fair."

"It's absolutely fair. But it would cost you a question to find out why. Speak carefully."

"OK. You say the joke's worth a question. So what is it that you find so hilarious?"

"You step on a plane in Albuquerque. Hours later you stumble through your door in the Pyrenees. You think you've traveled. In reality all that time you merely sat still while modes of transport ferried you about."

"That's what you find so funny?"

"I'll forgive you that question. In return, spare me further interruptions. I use you in a plane as an analogy. If that's too personal for comfort think of a pawn instead. This least significant member of a chess set has the potential to make it right across the board and become a queen. If it does so, should it be proud?"

"I suppose so."

"Ha! Some might say a little wooden chess piece has no consciousness, yet you're prepared to think one proud. This gets more hilarious by the moment. Tell me, why did I come here and meet you?"

"You said something about retrieving the young version of yourself. The boy Carlos. And something else about changing people's image of you."

"Ha ha ha. Perfect perfect perfect. You give pride to a chess piece and intentions to me."

"It's what you told me."

"Old habits die hard. All my life I freed my imagination to tell people what it would most excite them to hear."

"Do you mean you told lies?"

"I take that as a question. You have seven left. My answer is no. Lies are used to sustain fears. I have no fears. I told people stories to confirm their hopes of a more vibrant world. That vibrant world is real. My stories were the trains and planes to ferry them there. Now back to your original question. What is hilarious? This fact. That for a while, despite myself, I was convinced of the separate nature of my own existence."

"How—?"

He pushes his left hand toward me, palm out, urging me to stop.

"You throw me more questions when I am still answering? Please Martin, be patient. Do you want a fact to chew on? Here's one. We have dark and light, positive and negative, sweet and sour, none of which have meaning without the existence of their opposites. In the same way sorcerers always have doubles. In my life I would hear reports of what my double was up to. This duplicate of me took my name, took my appearance, even had hold of my memories. Try as they might, sorcerers never know what their doubles are up to. Stories filter back and we have to deal with the complications, but the double has always moved on. You spoke about fairness. Now is that fair, that our doubles have our memories and we don't have theirs?"

He looks at me, and grins.

"You have a question. It's written all over your face. Come on, out with it."

"Are you the double?"

"You ask me if I am my own double? The question is so funny I shan't count it."

"But you died. Why shouldn't your double carry on without you?"

"Take away light and there is no such concept as darkness. A sorcerer and his double are linked. Without one there is no other."

"Formlessness is no concept without form," I retaliate. I was tutored in abstruse philosophy and sometimes it shows. "Existence doesn't exist without nonexistence. A forgery cannot exist without an original, but when the original is destroyed the forgery can remain. You can have no double if you never existed, but when you died there's no reason your double couldn't carry on."

"So you win. I'm my own double. The point is not worth arguing. It makes no difference."

"It changes everything."

"How? You've shown no interest in me. Fake or original, I am what I am. You'll never know me. All our time together you've been interested in one thing: how I reflect on your experience."

"I can't get to know you. I can't even keep up with you. You keep changing all the time."

"I shimmer." He wags his head from side to side and holds something invisible between his hands which he moves like a wave from his head to his groin. "Your reflection is fractured. It's up to you to pull it together."

"What about you then? We went looking for your boy Carlos. What have you been pulling together?"

"You are using up a question to inquire about me?"

"Yes."

"I'm touched. I'd shed a tear if there were any left. But that tear you saw was my last. My boy Carlos has gone. You heard me calling him back. He rushed from me like a wind and there's no returning. What have I been pulling together? A dream of a new life. I borrowed some energy from you and felt it as my own. The thrill of nature raced through me on our valley walk. The return of my young Carlos almost burst me, it was so rich. It pumped me full of youth. Do you know what youth is?"

I shake my head.

"Youth is hope. Hope lives for a brighter future. Filled with my youth I longed for tomorrow. I readied myself for growth and change. The horror of it dawned on me as we were walking. Do you know the most terrifying aspect of being human?"

I don't bother to think, but simply shake my head again.

"Self-interest. And as I walked, brimming with youth, I felt self-interest rise in me. I had hopes. Better days were coming. It was worth saving myself to be a part of it. So I fled. Ran to this cave while I still knew the remedy. Made full body contact and poured my bubbling energy back into the earth."

"Are growth and change bad? Shouldn't we hope? Can't things get better?"

"Is that three questions?"

"Please answer it as one."

"I gave up hope long ago. I replaced it with thanksgiving. I appreciated everything as it is. I gave gratitude for still hanging around in my body. Everything is about relationship. In human terms we flourish when we are appreciated. It's the same with every aspect of life on Earth. Appreciation helps it flourish.

"I would sometimes drive up to Malibu and watch surfers crest the waves, hot young things feeling on top of the world. That image is my symbol for living in the moment. History is impossibly long. Take it back just to the creation of our universe, watch stars combust and dust congeal, see bacteria swirl and intermingle, mountains erupt from Earth's core and water coat its surface, through millions of years till oceans form and humans evolve and mothers give birth to children, till one child is born to swim into the Pacific and meet the breaking point of a particular wave. Imagine everything that has conspired to form that moment. An inexpressible tide of creation and destruction, change and growth. Can't you feel the wonder, that creation has been sustained so long that it has brought us to this point? A young man riding a wave.

"Another image. A woman sits in a laundromat, watching Oprah on TV while her family's clothes churn around in a machine. You've been there. You've seen it. Did you see the miracle it was? That the cosmos and beyond has conspired through all eternity to conjure up that moment? There is no greater miracle than that. And it happens everywhere, at all times.

"Take a worst-case scenario. Rain forests go the way of the dinosaurs, the human species follows. Imagine a moment beyond this disaster. Look at the landscape, look at the sky. Admire how much there is to be seen. Humanity came into being and passed out again to fertilize this moment. Think of the richness and wonder of that."

"Will it come to that?"

"Humans are sophisticated beings. It has become possible to imagine our own extinction. I can say this much. We have the power to save our species right now, but never in the future."

"That's a riddle, not an answer."

"Everything you'll ever hear is a riddle. It means nothing till you've worked it out in your own life. But I'll give you more. I'll tell you the most dynamic weapon in the whole human arsenal. It has the power of making anything you want come true. Are you ready for it?"

I nod my head.

"Are you sure? It's a big secret wrapped up in one word."

"I'm ready. Give me the word."

"Focus!"

It seems more of a damp squib than a bombshell. I look at him for further revelation. As he looks back I see movement in his eyes. First his right pupil wanders to the right. Then his left pupil floats to the left. As a technique it should be simple. It's simply the opposite of going cross-eyed. I've never seen the eyes cast wide in this way though. The effect is unnerving. I presume he's seeing double. For me the effect is different. As I look into his face I feel divided, as though two of me are seeing, one looking into each wayward eye.

His pupils wander back to the center, first the right and then the left. It's a relief. I smile to be released from his optical trick. I expect him to laugh, but he does nothing to either excuse or explain his actions. He simply speaks as though there has been no interruption.

"Whatever we focus on, that's what we get."

"So if we focus on the future, on a healthy planet, that's what we'll get?"

"Let's see, shall we?"

He shuffles forward till his legs are outside the cave and hanging down, and pats the ground to his right for me to join him.

"Look out there," he says when I am settled beside him.

I look across the meadow to the trees, to the movement of water in the river, to the surrounding mountains and the sky.

"Can you see it?" he asks.

"See what?"

"The future."

I stare some more.

"So where is it?" he persists.

"I don't know what you mean."

"Does the future happen here, or somewhere else?"

"Everywhere."

"Then it's here. Show it to me."

I look around the landscape but don't know what to do.

"Forget it, Martin. Forget the future. Believe in nothing you can't see."

"There are signs. Global warming. Corporate culture. Gaping holes in the ozone layer."

"You can see these things?"

"I see their effects. It's clear that if these trends continue our environment will be destroyed. Soon the trends will be irreversible."

"Do you lose sleep over this?"

"No. But I should."

"So you worry about not worrying enough?"

"When I think about it."

"Let me give you some perspective. Would you set an infant loose in a playground with a primed and loaded machine gun?"

"Of course not."

"Why? Because it knows how to use one?"

"No. Because it doesn't."

"Right. Yet we're all infants armed and set loose in the playground, turning our focus wherever we choose. Here's a scenario. You're strolling along a railroad and an express train is hurtling toward you. Do you focus on the train?"

"It sharpens my focus. I jump off the tracks."

"Good. Danger makes you focus, but you don't focus on the danger. You look at the ground beneath your feet. You move on. The train rushes by and there's no danger to it. Now I like rabbits more than squirrels. Squirrels are rodents. Rabbits are very like us. I'm speaking genetically, but it's clearest in the way rabbits face up to cars at night. They're great little runners, but they don't run. They are mesmerized by the headlights. Stand still and wait to be squashed. Their focus on the car wipes them out. Focus on the oncoming train and you're flattened. Focus on the destruction of the earth and you're history. Stop that, Martin!"

The sudden shout startles me. I'm doing nothing. Just sitting still.

"Stop what?"

"Fool. You've wasted a question. Stop waiting to have your say. Stop wanting to argue before you've even listened. If you must argue, keep waiting. Wait till I'm gone and go argue with the moon. There's no point to be won here. No point to be reached. It's all here. All now.

"You're a writer. Sit down to write a whole book in one go and you'd be paralyzed. That's not how it works. You focus on the next line, the next word. Are these your words? Think of the cosmos that created itself, created language, created you. Your choice of a word has been a long time coming. Maybe creation will sustain itself. Moment by moment, word by word, a book might appear. You say a pawn can be proud of becoming a queen? Then you can be proud of your book if you like. Or you can keep on living. Keep on paying attention to the work of each moment. If that work accumulates into something, so be it. It has its own existence. You're already in the next moment. You've moved on.

"Take a look through the opening. Who do you see out there?"

We had both shuffled back during the conversation, tucking ourselves inside the cave. I now look outside as directed and am dazzled by the light for a moment. Then the landscape becomes clear.

"Nobody."

"Par for the course. People don't care about Nature. Nature won't care about them."

"People are beginning to care."

"Impossible. You can't begin to care. If you truly care for one moment, you'll care the next. The power of wonder will have seized you. Focus on the future, even a do-gooding future, and you've missed it. The moment's gone by. You never noticed it. You're in a vacuum. Nature abhors a vacuum. It will wipe you out."

"So there's no hope."

"Never. There can be no hope. Hope is in the future. It never happens. But there is always a chance. While there's a person still living, there's a chance. Focus on the moment and it notices, it responds. The future will always take care of itself. Hang in there, appreciate it moment by moment, and it will include you."

. . .

I don't know how many moments we sit through, but it seems quite a while.

"Well?" Carlos asks. "What have you got to say for yourself?"

"Nothing comes to mind."

"Then this interview is over."

"But I've got more questions to ask."

"Not now. Please leave me for now. I prefer to be quiet."

"Will I see you again?"

"That's your ninth question—by a generous reckoning. I granted you ten. So long as you still have a question for me, you'll see me again."

"When—?"

"Don't be stupid." He puts his hand on my shoulder and pushes, urging me out of the cave. "Be quiet."

I climb down and walk across the meadow. The heat is fierce. The grass to my left and right is still, yet I feel a wind against my neck. I turn to look back at the cave, gaping in the hillside like an open mouth. This narrow wind is coming from that direction. I smile into it, and open my mouth to let it fill me.

People say winds die. I don't believe that happens. This wind stops and I stand and sweat. As I move again, walking back in the direction of my village and home, I find it waiting to glance its touch against my cheek.